DESIGNED
TO PROSPER

The Power of Biblical Principles

MARIA WATKINS

Scripture quotations marked NIV are taken from the Holy Bible, New International Version ®, NIV ® Copyright © 1973, 1978, 1984, 2011 by Biblica, Inc.Used with permission. All rights reserved worldwide.

Scripture quotations marked NKJV are from the New King James Version® Copyright© 1982, Thomas Nelson. All rights reserved.

1st edition 2025

Hardcover ISBN: 979-8-9921279-5-9
Paperback ISBN: 979-8-9921279-4-2
E-Book ISBN: 979-8-9921279-6-6

DEDICATION

This book is lovingly dedicated to my grandmother, Carmen Quintanilla, the first entrepreneur I ever knew. She was a woman of unshakable faith, relentless perseverance, and boundless love. She didn't just teach me about business, she showed me through her actions, through the way she carried herself, and through the unwavering determination in her spirit. She taught me how to sell, how to bargain, how to navigate both in the good and the bad times, but most importantly, she taught me how to trust God through it all.

I will never forget the way she would look at me, with eyes full of belief, as if she already saw the woman I would become. From a young age, she entrusted me to help her in her business, not just as a helper, but as someone she genuinely believed in and trusted. She poured into me with wisdom, patience, and faith, showing me that business was more than just making money, it was about resilience, integrity, and trusting in God's provision.

Looking back, I now realize that her prayers are the reason I am still here today. Her love was the anchor I didn't even know I needed, and her example shaped me in ways I am still discovering. She was, and will always be, the strongest woman I have ever known.

This book is dedicated to her, in gratitude for everything she taught me, for every lesson, every sacrifice, every silent prayer. I miss you, I love you, and I carry your legacy forward with honor. Thank you, Buelita Carmen.

ACKNOWLEDGEMENTS

To my two greatest blessings, Bentley and Carson. From the moment God placed you in my life, I knew you were destined for greatness. There is entrepreneurship running through your veins, a fire inside both of you that will one day blaze a trail for the Kingdom in ways beyond what we can see right now. You are not just my sons, you are future Kingdom builders, powerful vessels whom God will use mightily through business, leadership, and unshakable faith.

Thank you for believing in me, for standing by me with patience and understanding as I poured my heart into this book. I know there were moments when time with me felt shorter, when my focus was elsewhere, yet you never wavered in your support. You trusted me, even when the assignments God placed within my life didn't always make sense, even when they required sacrifices from all of us. You never questioned and never complained, you simply loved, encouraged, and covered me in prayer.

Your hugs, your words, and your unwavering presence have been my greatest strength. You remind me daily why I must run this race with excellence, because I know that everything I do, every battle I fight, every lesson I learn, is paving the way for your own journey of impact and purpose.

Bentley and Carson, I am so proud of you, and I thank God for you every single day. You are my greatest joy, my deepest inspiration, and the reason I will finish this race with my head held high, my heart full, and my purpose fulfilled. I love you both endlessly.

I would also like to acknowledge Ms. Bre. God sent you into my life for such a time as this, knowing exactly what I needed even when I didn't. You have given of yourself so selflessly, covering me in prayer, speaking life into me, and standing in the gap for me when I felt too weary to keep going. Without hesitation, without being asked, you interceded for me, poured encouragement into my spirit, and reminded me of the power of God's promises over my life.

You are the reason I started writing this book. Every time I wanted to stop, every time doubt crept in, I thought of your prayers, your prophesies and your unwavering faith. You believed in me when I struggled to believe in myself. You have been a vessel of God's love, wisdom, and strength, and because of your obedience, I have pressed forward when I otherwise might have quit.

I pray that the same love, faithfulness, and supernatural grace you have poured into me be returned to you a thousandfold in this lifetime. May you reap an abundant harvest from all that you have so selflessly sown. Thank you for being a light, a warrior, and a true reflection of God's heart. I am forever grateful.

CONTENTS

Dedication i

Acknowledgements iii

Introduction 1

PART 1: THE MINDSET OF A KINGDOM ENTREPRENEUR 5

Chapter 1   The Power of Stewardship Over Ownership 7

Chapter 2   The Law of Sowing and Reaping in Business 17

Chapter 3   Renewing Your Mind for Prosperity 27

PART 2: THE PRINCIPLES OF PROSPERITY 37

Chapter 4   Faith & Vision Seeing It Before It Happens 39

Chapter 5   The Law of Value Serving Before Selling 49

Chapter 6   The Law of Multiplication Scaling a Business God's Way 57

PART 3: LEADERSHIP & INFLUENCE 67

Chapter 7   Leadership That Glorifies God 69

Chapter 8   Integrity & Excellence in Business 79

Chapter 9   Faithful Finances Biblical Money Management 87

PART 4: TAKING ACTION & BUILDING LASTING PROSPERITY 103

Chapter 10   Overcoming Fear & Taking Risks in Faith 105

Chapter 11   Building Generational Wealth 117

Chapter 12   Scaling Your Business with Kingdom Impact 131

About the Author 141

INTRODUCTION

Have you ever felt like success was just out of reach, as if no matter how hard you worked, something was blocking your breakthrough? Maybe you've struggled with the idea of prosperity, wondering if it's even God's will for you to succeed. Let me settle that question right now, yes, it is.

God's desire for His people to prosper is woven throughout Scripture, but there's a difference between the prosperity the world chases and the prosperity God designed. The world defines success by status, wealth, and personal achievement, often attained at the expense of integrity, relationships, and inner peace. It pushes the idea that success must be seized through relentless hustle, self-promotion, and competition. However, true prosperity, the kind that comes from God, is built on a foundation of faith, stewardship, wisdom, and service. It is never just about money, it is about wholeness, impact, and legacy.

The Bible says, "Beloved, I pray that you may prosper in all things and be in health, just as your soul prospers." (3 John 1:2, NKJV). This scripture reveals God's heart: prosperity isn't limited to financial gain but extends to every area of life. It means flourishing spiritually, emotionally, relationally, and financially. It means operating in divine wisdom, making decisions led by faith rather than fear, and using wealth as a tool to fulfill God's purposes rather than chasing it for selfish gain.

Yet, many believers remain stuck, wrestling with the tension between faith and finances. Some have been conditioned to believe that poverty is more righteous than abundance. Others fear that wealth will corrupt them, or that business success is incompatible with a life devoted to God. But these are lies that have kept God's people bound for too long. From the beginning, God established principles of multiplication, stewardship, and financial wisdom. He placed Adam in the garden and told him to cultivate it, demonstrating that productivity and increase were always part of His design. Abraham was blessed beyond measure because of his faith and obedience. Joseph rose from prison to the palace because he applied divine wisdom in managing resources. The Proverbs 31 woman engaged in trade, made profitable investments, and provided for her household while honoring God in all she did. Even Jesus, in His teachings, spoke more about money, stewardship, and wise investments than nearly any other subject.

The issue has never been wealth itself, the issue is whether wealth controls you or whether you use it to serve God's purposes. Kingdom prosperity is about aligning with God's principles so that you can build something lasting, something that not only blesses you but also empowers others. It's about stepping into the fullness of what He has called you to do, with the divine resources, strategies, and wisdom to carry it out.

The principles in this book will challenge you to think differently about business, wealth, and success. They will equip you with the biblical mindset and practical strategies needed to create sustainable growth without compromising your faith. You will discover how to walk in divine wisdom, make sound financial decisions, lead with integrity, and multiply resources in a way that glorifies God.

If you have ever felt called to something greater but weren't sure how to move forward, this book is for you. If you've been stuck in cycles of financial struggle, doubt, or confusion, you are about to find clarity. If you've believed the lie that prosperity and righteousness cannot coexist, it's time to renew your mind and step into God's truth.

This is not just another book on prosperity. It is an invitation to build a life and business that reflect the heart of God, one that is prosperous, impactful, and rooted in eternal principles. Your journey to kingdom prosperity starts now.

Part 1

THE MINDSET OF A
KINGDOM ENTREPRENEUR

Success in the Kingdom of God does not start with money, connections, or even talent. It begins in the mind. The way a person thinks shapes their reality, influencing their decisions, actions, and ultimately, their results. The Bible declares, *"For as he thinks in his heart, so is he"* (Proverbs 23:7, NKJV). A person cannot consistently produce beyond the level of their mindset.

Kingdom entrepreneurship requires a renewed mind, one that is not confined by the limitations of the world's economic systems, fear-driven scarcity, or the belief that success is reserved for a select few. The world teaches that wealth is gained through relentless competition, self-serving ambition, and bending the rules to get ahead. God's system operates entirely differently. It is built on faith, integrity, and the supernatural favor that comes when a person aligns their business with His principles.

Many people desire success yet struggle to break through because they are bound by limiting beliefs. They may unknowingly carry a mindset shaped by past failures, generational poverty, or fear of stepping out in faith. These strongholds hinder their progress, keeping them in cycles of frustration, lack, and stagnation. A transformed mind is the key to breaking free from these strongholds and stepping into the prosperity God designed.

Kingdom entrepreneurs think differently. They see opportunities where others see obstacles. They rely upon God's wisdom rather than human reasoning. They understand that their business is not just a means of income, but a vehicle for impact, provision, and legacy. This level of thinking does not happen by accident. It is developed through intentional transformation, through aligning every thought with God's Truth.

The first step toward kingdom success is shifting from a mindset of limitation to one of expectation. God has already provided everything needed for those who will believe and take action upon their belief. His Word is filled with principles that lead to increase, yet many never experience this because they fail to renew their minds. The difference between those who prosper and those who struggle is not simply due to external circumstances but actually is due to the internal conditioning of their heart and mind.

In the coming chapters, the foundation of a kingdom entrepreneur's mindset will be laid out. Each principle will challenge old ways of thinking and introduce a new perspective rooted in biblical Truth. Those who embrace this transformation will not only experience personal breakthrough, they will also walk in the fullness of God's design for prosperity. A renewed mind is not just beneficial, it is essential!

1

THE POWER OF STEWARDSHIP
OVER OWNERSHIP

A Kingdom entrepreneur must first understand that everything belongs to God. The foundation of biblical success is not built on personal ownership but on faithful stewardship. *"The earth is the Lord's, and all its fullness, the world and those who dwell therein"* (Psalm 24:1, NKJV). Nothing in this world truly belongs to man. Wealth, resources, influence, and even life itself all originate from God. He entrusts people with these things, expecting them to manage them wisely according to His will.

However, the world operates with an ownership mentality, believing that personal achievements, hard work, and intelligence alone determine success. This mindset leads to pride, anxiety, and an endless pursuit of more. When people believe they are the sole owners of their business, they bear the full weight of its success and failures, often leading to stress, fear, and compromise. However, when a person shifts from an ownership mindset to a stewardship mindset, they can release control and walk in divine peace, knowing and trusting that God is the true source of their increase.

Stewarding Finances, Resources, and Relationships

Stewardship extends beyond finances. God entrusts His people with time, talents, opportunities, and relationships, all of which must be handled with wisdom. Every financial decision is an act of stewardship, determining whether a person is positioned for increase or unnecessary struggle. Jesus illustrated this in the Parable of the Talents (Matthew

25:14-30). The servant who managed his master's money wisely received greater responsibility and reward, while the one who buried his talent due to fear lost everything.

Money is never the goal in Kingdom business; it is a tool. A Kingdom entrepreneur must understand that wealth is a means of advancing God's purposes, blessing others, and breaking generational cycles of lack. When resources are stewarded well, they multiply. Wastefulness, on the other hand, leads to stagnation. This principle applies to more than just finances. Business relationships must also be stewarded with honor and integrity. Partnerships should be built on trust and mutual respect, reflecting Christ in every interaction. A business founded on manipulation, dishonesty, or self-serving ambition may prosper for a time, but it will not have lasting impact.

Time is another resource often mismanaged. Many believe that success is found in working harder, putting in excessive hours, and sacrificing their own well-being. While diligence is necessary, true stewardship means working with wisdom, seeking God's direction, and allowing Him to open doors that no amount of striving could achieve. Jesus operated in perfect timing. He never rushed, yet He fulfilled everything the Father called Him to do. When time is stewarded well, work becomes fruitful rather than exhausting.

The Difference Between Ownership and Stewardship Mentality

A person with an ownership mentality believes they must control every aspect of their business, relying solely upon their own efforts to produce success. This mindset leads to burnout, fear, and an attachment to material possessions. When things go wrong, anxiety and frustration take over, because the weight of responsibility rests entirely on human ability. This is not how God intended His people to live.

Stewardship, however, acknowledges that God is the true owner, and the role of His people is to manage what He has given wisely. This mindset brings freedom. A steward understands that if

God has called them to a business, He will provide for it. If a door closes, it is not the end of their business, it is simply a redirection. If challenges arise, they are opportunities for growth rather than reasons for fear. A steward does not cling to wealth but remains generous, knowing that provision comes from God, not from the business itself.

This principle is seen through Abraham's life. God blessed him abundantly, yet he remained a man of faith, willing to surrender anything when asked. When he was told to offer his son Isaac, he obeyed without hesitation, trusting in God's plan (Genesis 22:1-14). His willingness to release what he valued most demonstrated complete trust in the true Owner of all things. This is the heart of stewardship, trusting God's plan over personal control.

Trusting God's Ownership Brings Peace and Supernatural Favor

The shift from ownership to stewardship does not remove responsibility, but rather it places things in proper alignment. A Kingdom entrepreneur is still required to work, plan, and make wise decisions. However, they do so with the understanding that God is the source of their success. This mindset brings peace. Instead of being consumed by worry, a steward confidently moves forward, knowing that God provides wisdom, connections, and opportunities at the right time.

Supernatural favor follows those who recognize God as the true owner of their business. Joseph experienced this while managing Potiphar's house. Everything he touched prospered because he was a faithful steward. Even when he was unjustly imprisoned, God's favor remained on him, positioning him for elevation (Genesis 39:2-4, 21-23). His success was not based on circumstances but upon his unwavering commitment to stewarding what was entrusted to him.

A business built on Kingdom stewardship stands firm throughout economic downturns, shifts in the market, and unexpected challenges. The world's systems are unstable, constantly changing, and influenced by greed. A Kingdom entrepreneur who recognizes God as their provider will not be shaken, no matter what happens within the economy. The same God who fed Elijah through ravens, multiplied a widow's oil, and sustained the Israelites in the wilderness is the God who provides for His people still today.

Psalm 24:1 is not just a verse, it is a foundational principle. Everything belongs to the Lord, and those who walk in this truth experience a level of peace, provision, and success that the world cannot manufacture. A Kingdom entrepreneur does not chase wealth; they attract it through faithful stewardship. They do not fear loss; they trust that God will always supply. This is the power of living as a steward rather than as an owner.

The first step toward true Kingdom success begins with surrender, releasing the false sense of control and embracing the role of being a faithful steward. When this shift happens, the weight of stress lifts, fear loses its grip, and doors of opportunity begin to open in ways beyond anything human ability could achieve. This is how business is done in the Kingdom of God.

A Story of Ownership vs. Stewardship

Sophia Reynolds was the definition of success. She had built her marketing firm from the ground up, turning a one-woman operation into a thriving company with a team of employees, prestigious clients, and a reputation for excellence. People admired her drive, her discipline, and her ability to make things happen. Every award, every milestone, and every new contract reinforced the image she had worked so hard to create, a woman who had beaten the odds. What no one knew was the weight she carried.

Sophia's hunger for success had deep roots. She had grown up in a home where love was conditional, and safety was never guaranteed. Her father was absent, and her mother, trapped in her own struggles, often lashed out in anger. As a child, Sophia learned that if she wanted something, she had to fight for it. No one was coming to rescue her. She had spent years proving, first to herself, and then to the world, that she was worthy. Her business became her identity. It was her proof that she was in control, that she had overcome, that she would never be at the mercy of anyone again. Everything she built, she owned.

She didn't just run the business; she controlled every detail of it. She made every decision, handled every crisis, and trusted no one fully. Even though she had employees, she micromanaged them, convinced that if she didn't oversee every aspect, things would fall apart. She struggled to delegate, fearing that someone else would ruin what she had worked tirelessly to create.

Financially, she never felt secure, no matter how much she made. She saved aggressively, avoided risks, and never gave to charity or church. She had learned from childhood that holding onto resources was survival. Letting go, even in small ways, felt reckless to her. One day, after closing a major deal, Sophia sat in her office, looking at the numbers. It was her highest-earning quarter yet, however the anxiety in her chest had not lifted. The more she achieved, the heavier the burden became. The fear of losing what she had built consumed her.

A mentor had once told her, *"Sophia, if you think you own it, you have to sustain it. But if God owns it, He sustains it."* She had laughed it off then, but now the words haunted her.

That night, she found herself awake at 2 AM, scrolling through business articles, trying to quiet the unease she couldn't explain. She stumbled across a sermon about stewardship, and for the first time, she heard Psalm 24:1 in a way that hit her heart.

"The earth is the Lord's, and all its fullness, the world and those who dwell therein."

Tears welled up in her eyes. All its fullness. That meant everything she had: her business, her finances, even her very breath, was never truly hers. She had been acting as if success depended solely on her strength, her ability, and her relentless control. She had been living with an ownership mindset, gripping tightly onto something that was never meant to be held that way.

For the first time in years, she prayed, not a rushed, obligatory prayer, but a raw, honest one.

"God, I don't know how to let go. I don't know how to trust You with this. Show me how."

Over the next few weeks, she made small but radical changes. She began to delegate, trusting her team more and empowering them to lead. She tithed for the first time, feeling both terrified and free as she released control over her finances. She prayed over her business, not asking for more money, but for wisdom and alignment with God's purpose.

Something shifted.

The anxiety that had been a constant companion began to fade. Business decisions felt clearer, and unexpected opportunities started flowing her way. Clients she had been chasing for months suddenly reached out, new revenue streams opened, and for the first time, she felt peace, not because she had more money, but because she no longer carried the burden alone.

One evening, she received a call from a nonprofit she had donated to. They shared how her contribution had provided meals for struggling families. The woman on the phone, unaware of Sophia's story, simply said, *"Thank you for trusting God with what He's given you."* Sophia sat in silence after the call, realizing how much had changed in her heart. She was no longer just a successful entrepreneur. She was a steward.

The business was still thriving, but she no longer saw it as *hers*. It was God's, and she was simply managing it with wisdom and obedience. The difference was everything. She finally understood, when God owns it, He sustains it.

Biblical Principles of Stewardship Over Ownership

The following biblical principles will help reinforce the truths from this chapter. Meditate on these scriptures and apply them to your life and business as you walk in Kingdom stewardship.

1. **God Owns Everything** – *"The earth is the Lord's, and all its fullness, the world and those who dwell therein."* (Psalm 24:1, NKJV)

   o Recognizing that everything belongs to God removes the burden of ownership and allows you to steward with wisdom and peace.

2. **Faithful Stewardship Leads to Increase** – *"His lord said to him, 'Well done, good and faithful servant; you were faithful over a few things, I will make you ruler over many things. Enter into the joy of your lord.'"* (Matthew 25:23, NKJV)

   o God promotes those who steward well. Increase comes when you are faithful with what you have now.

3. **God Provides for Those Who Trust Him** – *"And my God shall supply all your need according to His riches in glory by Christ Jesus."* (Philippians 4:19, NKJV)

   o A Kingdom entrepreneur does not worry about lack because God is the ultimate provider.

4. **Stewardship Requires Wisdom and Planning** – *"Be diligent to know the state of your flocks, and attend to your herds; for riches are not forever, nor does a crown endure to all generations."* (Proverbs 27:23-24, NKJV)

   o Managing resources well includes financial responsibility, wise planning, and continual evaluation of your business and finances.

5. **God Blesses Those Who Honor Him with Their Resources** – *"Honor the LORD with your possessions, and with the*

firstfruits of all your increase; so your barns will be filled with plenty, and your vats will overflow with new wine." (Proverbs 3:9-10, NKJV)

  o Putting God first in business and finances leads to supernatural provision and overflow.

6. **Trusting God Removes Anxiety About Success** – *"Therefore do not worry, saying, 'What shall we eat?' or 'What shall we drink?' or 'What shall we wear?' For after all these things the Gentiles seek. For your heavenly Father knows that you need all these things. But seek first the kingdom of God and His righteousness, and all these things shall be added to you."* (Matthew 6:31-33, NKJV)

  o When you focus on God's Kingdom and righteousness, He ensures that everything you need is provided.

7. **Generosity is a Mark of a True Steward** – *"Give, and it will be given to you: good measure, pressed down, shaken together, and running over will be put into your bosom. For with the same measure that you use, it will be measured back to you."* (Luke 6:38, NKJV)

  o A steward understands that wealth is a tool to bless others, and generosity opens the door for greater increase.

8. **God's Favor Rests on Faithful Stewards** – *"The LORD was with Joseph, and he was a successful man; and he was in the house of his master the Egyptian."* (Genesis 39:2, NKJV)

  o When you are a faithful steward, God's presence and favor rest upon your business, causing it to prosper.

Applying These Principles

• Shift your mindset from ownership to stewardship by declaring daily that God is the true owner of your business and resources.

- Manage your finances, time, and relationships with wisdom, knowing that everything you have is entrusted to you by God.

- Release the stress of financial burdens by trusting in God's provision and seeking Him first.

- Practice generosity, knowing that giving is a key principle to Kingdom prosperity.

- Align every business decision with biblical integrity, trusting that God will bless and multiply what is handled righteously.

Meditate on these scriptures, pray over them, and begin applying them to your life and business. Stewardship is the foundation of Kingdom success, and those who embrace it will see the fullness of God's provision and favor. Many entrepreneurs, like Sophia Reynolds, fall into the trap of chasing the world's rewards rather than Heaven's. They pour everything into building something that was never meant to be carried by human strength alone. They strive, they stress, and they obsess over numbers, success, and security, only to find themselves running in circles, exhausted, anxious, and never truly satisfied.

The world teaches that success is about control, ownership, and accumulation, yet those who follow this path often end up with the very thing they feared most: emptiness. They believe that if they just achieve one more milestone, make one more dollar, or secure one more deal, they will finally feel at peace. Instead, they become slaves to their own success, bearing a weight they were never meant to carry. What so many fail to realize is that it was never theirs to begin with. It has always been God's.

The moment you shift from an ownership mindset to a stewardship mindset, everything changes. The weight lifts. The fear dissolves. You begin to walk in divine peace, knowing that God sustains what He owns. When you acknowledge Him as the true source, you no longer have to live in survival mode, gripping tightly to what was never meant to be held that way. Instead, you can build with confidence, knowing that every resource, opportunity and increase flows from His hand.

Let go of the illusion of control. Step into the freedom of stewardship. Trust that when you manage well what God has entrusted to you, He will not only sustain it, He will multiply it beyond what you could ever achieve on your own.

2

THE LAW OF SOWING AND REAPING IN BUSINESS

Every action, every decision, and every investment made in business operates under an unchangeable spiritual law: the law of sowing and reaping. This principle governs not only agriculture but also finances, relationships, leadership, and business growth. It is a divine system set in place by God Himself, ensuring that what a person plants, they will inevitably harvest.

The world operates under the illusion that success is random, dependent on luck or external circumstances. However, God's Word is clear that the outcomes in life and business are directly connected to what is sown. *"Do not be deceived, God is not mocked; for whatever a man sows, that he will also reap. For he who sows to his flesh will of the flesh reap corruption, but he who sows to the Spirit will of the Spirit reap everlasting life. And let us not grow weary while doing good, for in due season we shall reap if we do not lose heart."* (Galatians 6:7-9, NKJV).

Sowing Generously Produces Abundance

Many people desire a harvest without planting a seed. They want financial breakthrough without faithful giving, business success without diligence, and promotion without proving themselves trustworthy. This mindset contradicts the very nature of God's design. A farmer does not stand in an empty field and pray for a harvest without first putting seeds in the ground. The same is true in business, what is sown will determine what is reaped.

When seeds are planted in faith, a multiplied return follows. Jesus emphasized this in Luke 6:38, stating: *"Give, and it will be given to you: good measure, pressed down, shaken together, and running over will be put into your bosom. For with the same measure that you use, it will be measured back to you."* The level of generosity a person operates in determines the level of abundance received. Those who give sparingly will reap sparingly, but those who give bountifully will receive in abundance.

This principle applies not only to money but also to time, effort, and the value provided to others. A business that serves generously, offers exceptional quality, and operates with a spirit of excellence will experience greater return. Those who cut corners, give the bare minimum, or operate from a place of greed will find themselves struggling to sustain growth.

The Principle of Consistency in Sowing

The process of sowing and reaping does not produce instant results. A seed must go through a season of growth before it can yield fruit. Many give up too soon, expecting immediate rewards without allowing time for the results of their efforts to develop. This is why Galatians 6:9 urges believers to not grow weary while doing good, for in due season, the harvest will come.

Faithfulness in small actions leads to great impact over time. A business does not become successful overnight, and a financial breakthrough is rarely instantaneous. It is the daily decisions, the consistent acts of obedience, and the discipline to continue sowing that create lasting prosperity.

The world values overnight success, but the Kingdom of God values steady, faithful increase. The mustard seed, though the smallest of all seeds, grows into one of the largest trees because it follows God's process of development. Likewise, the consistent effort of a business owner who prioritizes integrity, service, and diligence will result in exponential growth over time.

Sowing in Faith, Not Fear

Fear hinders many from sowing. They hold onto resources tightly, believing that if they give, they will have less. This scarcity mindset contradicts Kingdom principles. In 2 Corinthians 9:6-8, the Bible states: *"But this I say: He who sows sparingly will also reap sparingly, and he who sows bountifully will also reap bountifully. So let each one give as he purposes in his heart, not grudgingly or of necessity; for God loves a cheerful giver. And God is able to make all grace abound toward you, that you, always having all sufficiency in all things, may have an abundance for every good work."*

A Kingdom entrepreneur does not operate in fear but in faith, trusting that whatever is given into the hands of God will be multiplied. Those who sow into their business, employees, and customers with generosity, excellence, and integrity will see supernatural increase. Those who operate in fear, withholding generosity and avoiding risks, often find themselves stuck in financial stagnation.

Understanding Seasons in Business

Every farmer knows there is a time to plant, a time to wait, and a time to harvest. Business operates the same way. There will be seasons of investment where effort seems greater than the reward. There will be seasons of waiting where growth is not immediately visible. However, just as a tree does not bear fruit the same day it is planted, financial increase follows a divine timeline.

Ecclesiastes 3:1 declares, *"To everything there is a season, a time for every purpose under heaven."* The key to thriving in business is recognizing which season you are in. If it is a time to sow, embrace the process with diligence. If it is a time of waiting, do not be discouraged. When the harvest comes, steward it well, knowing that new opportunities to sow will soon follow.

A person who understands this principle does not become frustrated when they do not see immediate results. Instead, they trust that God's promises are true and that every seed sown in faith will yield a return in due time.

The Cost of Holding Back

Jason Carter sat at his desk, staring at his business account balance. The numbers glowed back at him from the screen; there was just enough to cover expenses for the next two months. It wasn't much, but at least he wasn't drowning in debt.

He leaned back in his chair, rubbing his temples. Another opportunity had just come his way. A chance to invest in marketing that could expand his client base. It wasn't a gamble; it was a proven strategy that had helped others in his industry grow exponentially. The problem was, investing in it meant dipping into his savings, the little cushion he had left.

He closed the laptop and exhaled. "I can't risk it," he muttered to himself. "What if it doesn't work? What if I lose everything?"

Jason had always been cautious with money. Growing up in a home where financial struggles were constant, he had learned early on to hold onto whatever he had. His parents worked hard, yet every month, they barely made ends meet. They never gave to charity, rarely tithed, and always warned him about the dangers of taking financial risks. Their philosophy was simple: *You never know when you'll need it, so don't let go of what you have.*

Now, as a business owner, Jason found himself trapped in that same mentality. He avoided investments that required upfront capital. He hesitated to hire employees, afraid he wouldn't be able to afford their salaries. He rarely gave, even when he saw a need. When a struggling single mother in his church asked for help with groceries, he felt a tug in his heart, but his fear whispered louder: *If you give now, what if you don't have enough for yourself later?* So he had walked away, convincing himself that someone else would step in.

Months passed, and Jason's business remained stagnant. No matter how hard he worked, growth eluded him. He watched competitors, some who had even started after him, flourish while he struggled to maintain his small pool of clients. Every time he thought about the opportunities he had passed up, regret gnawed at him. He had played it safe, yet he was still stuck.

One evening, he attended a business conference where a well-known Christian entrepreneur shared his testimony. The speaker talked about how he had been in the same place as Jason, holding onto everything in fear of not having enough. Then one day, he read Galatians 6:7-9 and it changed his perspective.

"Do not be deceived, God is not mocked; for whatever a man sows, that he will also reap. For he who sows to his flesh will of the flesh reap corruption, but he who sows to the Spirit will of the Spirit reap everlasting life. And let us not grow weary while doing good, for in due season we shall reap if we do not lose heart."

The entrepreneur explained how he had started giving generously, investing in people, and sowing into his business even when it didn't make sense. Over time, he saw a supernatural return. Clients came from unexpected places, doors opened that he could never have orchestrated, and his finances multiplied.

Jason felt convicted. He had been expecting a harvest without planting any seeds. He had prayed for increase but had never sown in faith. Every decision had been rooted in fear, not trust.

That night, he went home and made a decision. The next morning, he called the marketing firm and signed the contract, finally investing in growth. He hired his first employee. For the first time, he tithed from his business revenue, not just from his personal income.

At first, nothing changed. The numbers still made him nervous. Fear still whispered that he had made a mistake. Yet, he chose to trust God's principle of sowing and reaping.

Three months later, everything shifted.

The marketing campaign paid off, and new clients flooded in. His employee's expertise took his business to a new level. Unexpected partnerships formed, opening doors he never anticipated. Jason saw firsthand that God honors faith-driven sowing. What he had feared losing, God had multiplied.

One day, as he stood in line at the grocery store, he noticed a woman struggling to pay for her food. She looked exhausted, and deeply embarrassed. Without hesitation, Jason stepped forward and covered her bill. She burst into tears, thanking him over and over again. As he walked away, he smiled. This time, there was no fear. He finally understood the truth, *when you sow in faith, you will always reap in abundance.*

Biblical Principles of Sowing and Reaping in Business

Below are the key biblical principles from this chapter. Meditate on these scriptures and apply them to your business to operate in divine abundance.

1. **What You Sow, You Will Reap** – *"Do not be deceived, God is not mocked; for whatever a man sows, that he will also reap."* (Galatians 6:7, NKJV)

    o Your results in business are directly tied to the seeds you plant, whether they be financial investments, acts of service, or leadership decisions.

2. **Sowing in Faith Leads to Increase** – *"Give, and it will be given to you: good measure, pressed down, shaken together,*

and running over will be put into your bosom. For with the same measure that you use, it will be measured back to you." (Luke 6:38, NKJV)

- o Generosity is the key to abundance. A Kingdom entrepreneur gives freely, knowing that God will provide in return.

3. **Do Not Grow Weary in Doing Good** – *"And let us not grow weary while doing good, for in due season we shall reap if we do not lose heart."* (Galatians 6:9, NKJV)

- o Faithfulness in small, consistent actions leads to breakthrough over time. Do not quit before your harvest arrives.

4. **God Loves a Cheerful Giver** – *"He who sows sparingly will also reap sparingly, and he who sows bountifully will also reap bountifully. So let each one give as he purposes in his heart, not grudgingly or of necessity; for God loves a cheerful giver."* (2 Corinthians 9:6-7, NKJV)

- o Giving should not be done out of obligation but with a joyful heart, trusting in God's abundance.

5. **There is a Season for Everything** – *"To everything there is a season, a time for every purpose under heaven."* (Ecclesiastes 3:1, NKJV)

- o Business operates in seasons. Recognize the times to sow, the times to wait, and the times to reap.

6. **Fear Blocks Increase, but Faith Multiplies** – *"For God has not given us a spirit of fear, but of power and of love and of a sound mind."* (2 Timothy 1:7, NKJV)

- o A business built on faith, not fear, experiences supernatural favor and multiplication.

Applying These Principles

- Assess what you are sowing daily in your business, whether through finances, service, or leadership.

- Stay faithful in your efforts, even when results are not immediate. The harvest will come in due season.

- Give generously, knowing that your provision comes from God, not your business alone.

- Operate in faith, trusting that God's timing is perfect and every seed planted will yield an abundant return.

By walking in the law of sowing and reaping, you align your business with Kingdom principles, ensuring lasting prosperity and divine success. The seeds you plant today will determine the harvest you experience tomorrow.

Jason's story is a testament to how quickly the principle of sowing and reaping can manifest in the natural. Within three months, his decision to step out in faith produced results beyond what he could have ever orchestrated on his own. His business expanded, doors of opportunity opened, and he experienced a new level of financial increase. However, not everyone sees their harvest this quickly. Some seeds take longer to bear fruit, requiring patience and endurance.

A farmer does not plant a seed and expect a full harvest overnight. Every seed undergoes an unseen process beneath the soil before it breaks through the surface. In the same way, the moment you sow, whether in your business, finances, relationships, or acts of generosity, growth begins, even if you cannot see it immediately. Seasons of waiting are not seasons of lack but seasons of preparation. The soil must be cultivated, the roots must strengthen, and the conditions must align for the harvest to fully develop.

Rest assured, the law of sowing and reaping is as certain as the rising of the sun. If a seed has been planted, fruit is growing. Whether it manifests in three months, three years, or beyond, the Word of God promises that in due season, you will reap if you do not lose heart. Trust in the process, continue sowing in faith, and expect a harvest that far exceeds what you planted. The Kingdom operates on divine timing, and those who persist will experience supernatural increase.

3

RENEWING YOUR MIND FOR PROSPERITY

Success in business, finances, and in life is first won or lost in the mind. A person's thoughts shape their beliefs, and their beliefs dictate their actions. Many people desire prosperity but remain trapped in cycles of lack, fear, and struggle, not because they lack opportunity, but because their mindset has never been renewed. The Bible makes it clear that transformation begins in the mind:

"And do not be conformed to this world, but be transformed by the renewing of your mind, that you may prove what is that good and acceptable and perfect will of God." (Romans 12:2, NKJV)

The world has conditioned people to think in ways that directly oppose God's principles. From an early age, many are taught to fear financial instability, to see wealth as something only a select few attain, or to believe that success must come through relentless struggle. Some have been raised in poverty, developing a mindset that says, *"This is just how life is."* Others have been surrounded by doubt and discouragement, causing them to settle for less than what God intends. Yet, God's Word calls for a radical transformation, a complete renewal of the mind.

Breaking Free from Limiting Beliefs

Many people unknowingly carry limiting beliefs that hinder their ability to prosper. These beliefs stem from past experiences, cultural conditioning, and even well-meaning family influences. A person who grew up hearing *"money is the root of all evil"* (a misinterpretation of

1 Timothy 6:10) may subconsciously reject financial success, fearing that wealth will corrupt them. While someone who has experienced repeated failure may believe they are simply "not meant" to succeed, failing to realize that setbacks are often stepping stones to even greater opportunities.

Limiting beliefs operate as strongholds: mental barriers that keep people trapped in cycles of lack, fear, and stagnation. Scripture instructs believers to demolish these strongholds:

"For the weapons of our warfare are not carnal but mighty in God for pulling down strongholds, casting down arguments and every high thing that exalts itself against the knowledge of God, bringing every thought into captivity to the obedience of Christ." (2 Corinthians 10:4-5, NKJV)

Every thought that contradicts God's truth must be confronted and replaced with what He says. Renewing the mind requires a conscious decision to reject fear, doubt, and scarcity thinking and to embrace faith, abundance, and expectation.

Developing a Kingdom Prosperity Mindset

The world operates on a scarcity mindset, convincing people that resources are limited, competition is necessary, and success comes at the expense of others. The Kingdom of God, however, functions on principles of abundance. God is not limited by the economy, business trends, or human limitations. His provision is limitless, and His desire is to bless His people so they can be a blessing to others.

A renewed mind embraces the reality that:

- **God is the source of all provision** – *"And my God shall supply all your need according to His riches in glory by Christ Jesus."* (Philippians 4:19, NKJV)

28

- **We are heirs to God's abundance** – *"The blessing of the Lord makes one rich, and He adds no sorrow with it."* (Proverbs 10:22, NKJV)

- **Prosperity is not about selfish gain but about fulfilling God's purposes** – *"You shall remember the LORD your God, for it is He who gives you power to get wealth, that He may establish His covenant which He swore to your fathers, as it is this day."* (Deuteronomy 8:18, NKJV)

When a person shifts from a scarcity mindset to an abundance mindset, they no longer see success as something out of reach. They recognize that prosperity is not about luck or privilege, it is about aligning with biblical principles, making wise decisions, and trusting God's plan.

Aligning Thoughts with Actions

Many people have dreams of financial freedom, business success, and making an impact, yet their daily actions prevent the fulfillment of these desires. They may want to build a successful business, yet they procrastinate, refuse to invest in learning, and/or allow fear to hold them back. They may desire financial increase, yet they avoid taking financial risks, hold onto a poverty mentality, or fail to operate in generosity.

Renewing the mind is not just about changing thoughts. It requires aligning thoughts with actions.

- A person who believes in prosperity but refuses to step out in faith remains stagnant.

- A business owner who desires success but refuses to develop skills, invest in mentorship, or take bold actions will never grow their business or finances.

- Someone who dreams of financial freedom but refuses to steward their money wisely will remain in a financial struggle.

Faith without action is dead (James 2:26). A renewed mind leads to renewed habits, decisions, and discipline.

The Battle in the Mind

Madison sat in her car, staring at the entrance of her office building, paralyzed by the weight of her thoughts. She had been battling the same cycle for years: doubt, fear, and the overwhelming feeling that she wasn't good enough. No matter how much success she achieved, a voice in the back of her mind whispered, *"You don't belong here. You're not capable. You will fail, just like before."*

She had grown up believing she wasn't smart enough, strong enough, or worthy enough to achieve anything great. Those words had been spoken over her in childhood, and they had shaped the way she saw herself. Every rejection, every failure, and every hard moment simply reinforced what she already believed: *I'm not enough.*

Even as she grew older and built her career, those lies remained. She had tried to ignore them, push through them and prove them wrong, but no matter how much she accomplished, the feelings of inadequacy never left. One Sunday, while scrolling through social media, she saw a quote from a sermon: *"If you don't take control of your thoughts, they will control you."* It struck something deep within her. She knew that the battle she faced wasn't external; it was in her mind. That night, she opened her Bible, desperate for something, anything, to break the cycle. She came across Romans 12:2 which states:

"And do not be conformed to this world, but be transformed by the renewing of your mind, that you may prove what is that good and acceptable and perfect will of God." (Romans 12:2, NKJV)

She read it again. And again. Could it be that the life she was living: the fear, the self-doubt, the anxiety, was a result of the thoughts she had been feeding? Could it be that she had accepted lies as truth for so long that she had allowed them to shape her entire life?

That night, she made a decision. She wasn't going to live another day believing the enemy's lies. She was going to renew her mind.

At first, it felt impossible. The moment she woke up, the negative thoughts were there, just as strong as ever. "You're not enough. You're going to fail. No one believes in you." This time though, she did something different. Instead of accepting those thoughts, she challenged them.

When the thought came, *"You're not enough,"* she spoke out loud:
"I can do all things through Christ who strengthens me." (Philippians 4:13, NKJV)

When the thought came, *"You are going to fail,"* she declared:
"For God has not given us a spirit of fear, but of power and of love and of a sound mind." (2 Timothy 1:7, NKJV)

When the thought came, *"No one believes in you,"* she reminded herself:
"If God is for us, who can be against us?" (Romans 8:31, NKJV)

At first, it felt awkward, even forced. Speaking Scripture out loud was not something she was used to doing. The lies felt so ingrained in her mind that the truth seemed foreign. Yet, she had made a commitment: she would not let the enemy have her mind. Days turned into weeks, and Madison continued the battle. Some days were easier than others. Some mornings she woke up with a sense of peace, and other mornings the war in her mind felt relentless.

There were moments she felt exhausted, wondering if she would ever fully believe the Truth she was speaking over herself. Yet, every time she spoke God's Word, it was like planting a seed. At first, nothing seemed to change, but deep within, something was shifting. Then, one day, she realized something. She walked into a meeting with confidence, without second-guessing herself. She made a bold business decision without fear. She turned down an opportunity that didn't align with God's will, trusting that He had something better.

It wasn't an overnight transformation, but it was happening. She was proving what Romans 12:2 said—she was being transformed by the renewing of her mind.

Madison learned a powerful truth: the mind is the main battlefield of the enemy. The devil doesn't need to take your finances, your relationships, or your career to destroy you. All he needs is access to your thoughts. If he can keep you believing lies, doubting yourself, and fearing the future, he knows you will never fully step into what God has destined for you.

The enemy works in deception, planting subtle thoughts that seem harmless at first. *"You're not good enough. No one cares. You will never succeed."* If those thoughts are not confronted, they take root and begin shaping your actions, decisions, and destiny.

Yet, God's Word is clear: We have the power to take every thought captive.

"For the weapons of our warfare are not carnal but mighty in God for pulling down strongholds, casting down arguments and every high thing that exalts itself against the knowledge of God, bringing every thought into captivity to the obedience of Christ." (2 Corinthians 10:4-5, NKJV)

A person cannot expect to walk in Kingdom prosperity while holding onto thoughts that oppose the Truth of God. Every stronghold must be torn down, every lie replaced, and every thought brought into obedience.

Madison's story is not unique. Many people live their entire lives imprisoned by their own thoughts, never realizing they have the power to be free. The renewing of the mind is not a one-time event; it is a daily process, a lifelong commitment to choosing truth over deception. Some days, the battle will be intense. The lies will try to creep back in. Yet, for those who persist, for those who continually replace lies with God's Word, transformation is inevitable.

The mind is the gateway to fulfilling everything God has planned. If your thoughts are aligned with His Truth, there is nothing that can stop you from walking in the fullness of your destiny. The choice is yours, live bound by lies or be transformed by Truth.

Biblical Principles for Renewing Your Mind for Prosperity

Below are key scriptures and principles that will help you renew your mind and align your business with Kingdom prosperity:

1. **Transformation Begins in the Mind** – *"And do not be conformed to this world, but be transformed by the renewing of your mind, that you may prove what is that good and acceptable and perfect will of God."* (Romans 12:2, NKJV)

   o Your thoughts determine your reality. Renewing your mind with God's Truth is the first step toward prosperity.

2. **Break Free from Limiting Beliefs** – *"For the weapons of our warfare are not carnal but mighty in God for pulling down strongholds."* (2 Corinthians 10:4, NKJV)

   o Every thought that contradicts God's promises must be cast down and replaced with His Truth.

3. **God is the Source of All Provision** – *"And my God shall supply all your need according to His riches in glory by Christ Jesus."* (Philippians 4:19, NKJV)

    o True prosperity comes from trusting God as your provider, not relying on human effort alone.

4. **Faith Without Action is Dead** – *"For as the body without the spirit is dead, so faith without works is dead also."* (James 2:26, NKJV)

    o Renewing the mind requires aligning thoughts with action to produce real results.

Applying These Principles

- Identify and replace limiting beliefs that hinder your success.

- Trust God as your source, rather than living in fear of lack with a poverty mindset.

- Align your actions with your renewed mindset, take faith-driven steps toward prosperity.

Renewing your mind is not optional, it is a requirement for walking in the fullness of what God has destined for you. Without renewing your mind, the enemy will keep you bound in fear, doubt, and limitation. The greatest battle you will ever fight is the battle for your mind, and if you do not take control of your thoughts, they will control you.

You were never created to live in cycles of defeat. You were never meant to struggle with insecurity, fear, or scarcity. God has called you to prosper, but prosperity starts in your mind before it ever manifests in your life. If you think small, you will live small. If you believe lies, you will stay trapped in them. If you allow fear to dictate your choices, you will never step into the abundance God has prepared for you.

Yet, you are not powerless. God has given you the tools to tear down strongholds, break generational mindsets, and step into a completely transformed life. It begins with a decision to reject every thought that contradicts God's Word and replace it with His Truth.

The process will not always be easy, but it will be worth it. Some days will feel like a battle, and old thoughts may try to creep back in. Yet, for those who persist, those who commit to daily renewal, and those who refuse to let the enemy have dominion over their minds, transformation is inevitable.

Your mind is the gateway to your destiny. If you align your thoughts with Heaven, nothing can stop you from walking in the prosperity, success, and purpose that God has ordained for you. It is time to take your thoughts captive. It is time to replace every lie with truth. It is time to renew your mind and step into Kingdom prosperity. The choice is yours. Will you stay bound by the past, or will you step into the future God has called you to?

Part 2

THE PRINCIPLES OF PROSPERITY

Prosperity is not an accident. It is not reserved for a select few, nor is it the result of random luck or chance. True prosperity is a divine process, governed by principles which, when understood and applied, unlock a life of abundance, purpose, and impact. God did not design His children to live in lack, constantly striving and never arriving. He created them to flourish, to expand, to multiply, and to steward resources in a way that brings both personal fulfillment and Kingdom advancement.

Many people desire financial freedom, but few truly understand the principles that govern prosperity. The world defines wealth by what is accumulated: bank accounts filled, businesses scaled, and assets increased. Yet, biblical prosperity is not just about wealth; it is about wholeness. It is about walking in the fullness of God's provision, not just for personal comfort but for divine purpose. The wealth of the wicked may be built upon deception, manipulation, or greed, but Kingdom prosperity is built upon integrity, generosity, and alignment with God's will.

This section will reveal the divine laws that govern increase, laws that are as unshakable as gravity and as reliable as the rising sun. These principles are not just spiritual ideals; they are practical, actionable truths that transform businesses, families, and entire generations. When applied, they shift mindsets, open doors of opportunity, and position believers to operate in the overflow of God's provision.

The principle of faith and vision will challenge you to see beyond your present circumstances and step into the future God has planned for you. The principle of value and service will reveal how true wealth is created, not by chasing money, but by solving problems, meeting needs, and serving others with excellence. The principle of multiplication will unveil how God intends for everything in your hands to increase, ensuring that what you build does not end with you but expands far beyond your lifetime.

These are not temporary strategies. These are eternal Truths, designed by the Creator of all things. Those who embrace them will rise above the limits of the world's economic systems and step into supernatural provision. The difference between those who prosper and those who struggle is not luck; it is revelation. Once you grasp these principles, you will never look at business, money, or success the same way again.

Get ready. The principles of prosperity are about to be unlocked, and when they are, nothing will be able to stop what God is preparing to release in your life.

4

FAITH & VISION
SEEING IT BEFORE IT HAPPENS

Everything that exists in the natural realm was first created in the unseen realm. Every building was once a blueprint, every invention was once an idea, and every business was once a vision in someone's mind before it became a reality. Nothing manifests without first being conceived internally. The principle of faith and vision is the foundation of every great move of God, every breakthrough in business, and every step into prosperity.

Proverbs 29:18 declares, *"Where there is no revelation, the people cast off restraint; but happy is he who keeps the law."* (NKJV). Other translations state, *"Where there is no vision, the people perish."* (KJV) Vision is not optional, it is necessary. Without it, people wander aimlessly, making decisions based on their circumstances rather than upon divine purpose. Without vision, businesses fail, families lose direction, and individuals remain stuck in mediocrity. Vision is the spiritual blueprint for everything God desires to bring into existence.

The Mind's Ability to Shape Reality

God designed the human mind with the supernatural ability to create, envision, and bring the unseen into reality. Imagination is not a childish exercise, rather it is the very tool God has given man to conceive and manifest His plans. The enemy has worked tirelessly to corrupt man's imagination, filling minds with doubt, fear, and "worst-case scenarios", because he knows that if people ever understood the true power of their God-given imagination, they would begin walking in supernatural faith.

Andrew Wommack, in *The Power of the Imagination*, explains that imagination is the "incubator of faith". A person cannot believe for something they have never first pictured in their mind. Everything starts with an image. When God told Abraham he would be the father of many nations, He gave him a visual representation, stars in the sky, to keep before his eyes. Abraham had to see it before he could receive it. The same principle applies today. What is continually meditated upon, visualized, and imagined will eventually manifest.

A person who constantly imagines failure, loss, and struggle will inevitably walk in those things. Someone who trains their imagination to see God's promises, financial abundance, supernatural success, and Kingdom impact will experience those things in their life. Faith is not blind; it sees what others cannot yet perceive.

Faith Requires Seeing Before Receiving

Faith is the ability to believe in what the natural eyes cannot yet see. Hebrews 11:1 states, *"Now faith is the substance of things hoped for, the evidence of things not seen."* (NKJV). This means that faith gives substance to the invisible. Without faith, nothing can be manifested in the natural realm.

Jesus consistently taught the principle of seeing before receiving. When He stood before the tomb of Lazarus, He thanked God for hearing Him *before* the miracle happened (John 11:41-44). When He fed the five thousand, He blessed the loaves and fishes *before* they multiplied (Matthew 14:19-21). He always acted as though what He saw in the spirit was more real than what existed in the natural. Many believers struggle in business and finances because they only operate from what they see with only their physical eyes. They react to circumstances instead of walking by faith. A Kingdom entrepreneur does not wait for the manifestation of a thing before believing, it is believed first, imagined in vivid detail, and then received.

The Vision Must Be Written and Declared

God instructed Habakkuk, *"Write the vision and make it plain on tablets, that he may run who reads it."* (Habakkuk 2:2, NKJV). What you envision must be recorded, spoken, and reinforced daily. Those who leave their dreams in their minds, without putting them into tangible form, rarely see them come to pass. Writing down a vision is a prophetic act. It declares that what is currently unseen will soon be established.

Speaking the vision out loud is just as important. *"Death and life are in the power of the tongue, and those who love it will eat its fruit."* (Proverbs 18:21, NKJV). Spoken words create reality. What is repeatedly spoken will begin to shape thoughts, expectations, and actions. Successful Kingdom entrepreneurs declare God's promises over their business, finances, and future. They speak increase, favor, and divine strategies into existence.

Imagination Activates the Supernatural

The imagination is the bridge between the spiritual and the physical. Many pray for miracles, but few take the time to truly imagine them happening. If a person prays for financial increase yet constantly envisions bills piling up, they are canceling out their faith with doubt. True faith requires seeing the miracle before it manifests.

This principle is why Jesus often asked people what they wanted before healing them. He wanted them to see it internally before experiencing it externally. In Mark 10:51, He asked the blind man, *"What do you want Me to do for you?"* (NKJV). It wasn't because He didn't know, it was because He needed the man to picture himself healed.

If a business owner envisions failure more than success, it is only a matter of time before their reality aligns with their dominant thoughts. If an entrepreneur cannot see themselves leading a successful company, hiring employees, expanding their reach, and being financially free, they will struggle to achieve it. God partners with our faith-filled imagination to bring supernatural results.

Biblical Examples of Vision Bringing Prosperity

Throughout Scripture, those who experienced great success first had a vision:

- **Joseph** saw himself as a ruler long before he stood before Pharaoh. His dreams gave him the endurance to go through betrayal, false accusations, and imprisonment. Without a vision, he would have lost hope in the process (Genesis 37:5-10).

- **Moses** led the Israelites toward the Promised Land because he believed in the vision God gave him. Though the people complained and doubted, Moses never wavered in his belief that they would inherit what was promised (Exodus 3:7-10).

- **David** was anointed as king while still a shepherd. Long before he took the throne, he carried the vision in his heart. Despite years of hiding from Saul and facing opposition, he never lost sight of what God had spoken (1 Samuel 16:12-13).

A Story of Faith and Imagination

James had lived his entire life bound by the chains of a mindset he never chose. Raised by his grandmother, he had been fed a steady diet of entitlement and blamelessness. She always reassured him that nothing was ever his fault. If he failed, it was because someone else had cheated him. If he struggled, it was because the world was against him. If he didn't succeed, it was because rich and powerful people made sure people like him never would succeed.

"You work hard, and what do you get?" she would mutter, shaking her head as she watched the evening news. "Nothing. They take it all. That's why we stay where we are. It's not your fault, baby. It's just the way the world is."

Her words sank deep into James' subconscious, shaping the way he saw himself and his future. His biological parents weren't involved in his life, and neither of them had ever shown any real ambition. His mother was always just barely getting by, working jobs she hated, and his father was someone he only knew by name. Neither of them had ever talked about dreams or vision. They merely existed; James learned to do the same.

As a teenager, he never dreamed of being anything greater. When teachers encouraged students to think about their future careers, James shrugged. "What's the point?" he thought. "I'll just get stuck in some job I hate, barely making enough to live." By the time he was old enough to work, his attitude was set. He expected the world to give him what he deserved. When he got a job at a hardware store, he worked with minimal effort, constantly complaining about the low wages. "They should pay me more," he'd say, leaning against the counter when customers weren't around. "They make so much money off us, and we get nothing."

When he was reprimanded for slacking off, he blamed the manager for being too demanding. When he was passed over for a promotion, he convinced himself it was favoritism. He never considered that his own attitude and lack of initiative might have played a role. His imagination had been hijacked by limitation, and all he could see was a future of struggle. He imagined himself always being stuck, always being overlooked, always being in the same place, so that is exactly where he remained.

One evening, after another frustrating day, James wandered into a small diner, intending to drown his irritation in a cup of coffee. As he sat there, lost in thought, he overheard a conversation at the booth behind him. A deep, steady voice spoke with authority, cutting through the noise of the restaurant.

"I'm telling you, the only limits in life are the ones you accept. If you can't see yourself walking in something greater, you never will."

James turned, slightly intrigued. The speaker was an older man, his presence commanding yet peaceful. His name was Samuel, and he was well-known in the community as a businessman and mentor. Something about his words stirred something deep within James, something uncomfortable, yet strangely compelling. Without fully thinking it through, James stood up and approached the man's booth. "Excuse me, sir," he said hesitantly. "I heard what you were saying about limits. I don't really understand what you mean."

Samuel looked up, studying James for a moment before gesturing for him to sit down. "Tell me about yourself," he said. James hesitated before sharing bits and pieces of his life, his struggles, his frustrations, how nothing ever seemed to work out for him. He expected Samuel to nod in sympathy, to affirm what his grandmother had always told him, that life had been unfair to him. Instead, the man leaned forward, his eyes sharp with conviction.

"Son, your problem isn't your past. It's not your family, your job, or even the world around you. Your real problem is that you've never seen anything different."

James frowned. "What do you mean?"

Samuel pulled a small notebook from his pocket and flipped to a passage, then read aloud: *"Where there is no revelation, the people cast off restraint; but happy is he who keeps the law."* (Proverbs 29:18, NKJV).

"This means that if you can't see a future beyond where you are, you'll never move towards it. You've spent your whole life imagining failure, so that's all you ever walk in. You've been using your imagination against yourself."

James stared at him, confused. "I don't even think I have an imagination."

Samuel chuckled. "Oh, you do. Everyone does. Right now, you're probably picturing yourself stuck in the same dead-end life you've always had, aren't you?"

James nodded slowly.

"That's your imagination," Samuel said. "And it's working against you. God gave you the ability to see before you step into something. If all you see is lack, struggle, and limitations, that's all you'll ever experience. However, if you start seeing yourself as capable, as successful, as someone walking in God's purpose, everything will begin to change." The words hit James like a lightning bolt! He had never considered that his own thoughts were working against him; that his imagination was actively reinforcing the life he hated.

Samuel saw the shift happening in James' eyes and smiled. "I want to mentor you. If you're willing, I'll show you how to renew your mind with God's Word; how to use your imagination to shape your future instead of sabotage it."

James hesitated, and then nodded. "I don't want to stay stuck," he admitted. "I just don't know how to change."

"Good," Samuel said. "That means you're ready."

From that day forward, James' life began to transform. Samuel taught him how to see his life through the eyes of faith, how to envision success before it happened. Every morning, James wrote down what he wanted his future to look like, picturing himself as a leader, an entrepreneur, and a man of faith.

The more he envisioned success, the more his actions changed. He stopped complaining and started taking initiative at work. He stopped waiting for someone to give him something and started learning skills on his own. He imagined himself as someone who could build something greater, and soon, the opportunities to do so started appearing.

Within two years, he had started his own business, something he once thought was impossible. Within five years, he was hiring employees and mentoring young men who reminded him of his previous self. The difference? He had learned to see beyond where he was.

James realized that prosperity had never been out of reach. The only thing that had kept him from stepping into it was his own limited vision. Once he learned to see himself the way God saw him, he was able to step into the reality that had been waiting for him all along. James was no longer merely a victim of circumstance; he was an overcomer. He was a man of faith and vision.

Biblical Principles of Faith & Vision

The following scriptures and principles reinforce the power of faith and vision. Meditate on them and apply them to your life and business:

1. **Without Vision, People Perish** – *"Where there is no revelation, the people cast off restraint; but happy is he who keeps the law."* (Proverbs 29:18, NKJV)

   o A clear vision brings purpose, direction, and discipline. Without it, people remain stuck in cycles of uncertainty.

2. **Faith is the Evidence of the Unseen** – *"Now faith is the substance of things hoped for, the evidence of things not seen."* (Hebrews 11:1, NKJV)

   o Faith sees what does not yet exist and brings it into reality.

3. **Write the Vision and Speak It** – *"Write the vision and make it plain on tablets, that he may run who reads it."* (Habakkuk 2:2, NKJV)

    o A vision should be written down, reviewed daily, and spoken outloud with faith.

4. **God Works Through Our Imagination** – *"Then He brought him outside and said, 'Look now toward heaven, and count the stars if you are able to number them.' And He said to him, 'So shall your descendants be.'"* (Genesis 15:5, NKJV)

    o God gave Abraham a picture of His promise, reinforcing the power of imagination.

5. **Speak Life Over Your Vision** – *"Death and life are in the power of the tongue, and those who love it will eat its fruit."* (Proverbs 18:21, NKJV)

    o Words create reality. Speak life over your business and future.

Applying These Principles

- Take time daily to visualize your success, seeing it in your mind before it manifests.

- Write down your vision, read it daily and declare it out loud.

- Remove negative thoughts and replace them with faith-filled imagination.

- Ask God to reveal the vision He has for your business and align your actions with His plan.

James' story is not unique. Every person is either living in the vision they have cultivated or the one they have neglected. The ability to see beyond current circumstances is not just a skill, it is a necessity for stepping into the fullness of God's plans. Faith and vision are inseparable, and imagination is the bridge between the unseen and the tangible. God has already designed a future for you, one filled with purpose, provision, and impact. The question is not whether it exists, the question is whether you can see it. What you allow your mind to dwell on, what you choose to envision daily, will determine what manifests in your life. If you continue to see yourself limited, struggling, and trapped, you will remain there. If you dare to see yourself walking in the abundance God has prepared, you will begin moving in that direction. The key is learning to align your imagination with faith, seeing what God has spoken before it happens, speaking what He has promised before it manifests, and walking towards it with confidence. This is the foundation of supernatural prosperity, and it is only the beginning.

The next principle of prosperity will take this even further, revealing how value and service multiply wealth, how problem-solving unlocks doors, and how true prosperity is not about chasing money but about creating impact. If you are ready to shift from survival mode to overflow, from wishing to walking, then what comes next will change everything for you.

5

THE LAW OF VALUE
SERVING BEFORE SELLING

In the world's system, success is often measured by how many people serve you, how much wealth you accumulate, and how much power you can exert over others. The higher you climb, the more you are revered. The world teaches that to be great, you must make yourself known, assert dominance, and position yourself where others are beneath you.

God's Kingdom operates in the exact opposite manner. In His system, true greatness is not found in how many people serve you, but in how well you serve others. Increase does not come from selfish ambition but from selfless contribution. Promotion in the Kingdom is not about how much you take but about how much you give. Jesus Himself laid out this principle clearly:

"Yet it shall not be so among you; but whoever desires to become great among you, let him be your servant. And whoever desires to be first among you, let him be your slave—just as the Son of Man did not come to be served, but to serve, and to give His life a ransom for many." (Matthew 20:26-28, NKJV)

This principle is the foundation of true success. If you desire to rise in business, influence, or leadership, you must first embrace servanthood. If you want financial increase, you must first focus on how you can add value to others. If you want to be entrusted with more, you must first be faithful with what you have.

Going Low to Go High, The Path of Humility

Jesus taught that the way up is down. The path to true greatness begins with humility.

"And whoever exalts himself will be humbled, and he who humbles himself will be exalted." (Matthew 23:12, NKJV)

Pride is the greatest enemy of true success while humility is the foundation for lasting prosperity. Many people seek to be recognized, to be honored, to be respected, and to be served, but few are willing to lower themselves to serve first. The world will tell you to chase power, but God will tell you to lay it down and watch Him lift you up in due time.

Joseph was destined for greatness, yet his journey to the palace started in the pit, then slavery, and later, a prison cell. He did not arrive at his place of leadership by demanding authority but by proving himself faithful in every stage of servitude (Genesis 39:2-4, 21-23). Before he ruled over Egypt, he served in Potiphar's house. Before he saved a nation, he interpreted the dreams of prisoners. His promotion came because he embraced servanthood before kingship.

David was anointed as king, yet his first assignment after being chosen and anointed king was to continue tending sheep. Before he ever ruled a nation, he served Saul, played music for him, and even carried food to his brothers on the battlefield (1 Samuel 16:11-13, 19-23; 17:17-18). He did not take the throne through force, he waited in humility, and God elevated him in the right season.

Jesus, the King of Kings, demonstrated this principle of humble service most powerfully. The night before His crucifixion, He stooped down to wash the feet of His disciples, taking the position of a servant (John 13:3-5). If the Son of God Himself modeled humility, no entrepreneur, leader, or businessperson is exempt. True prosperity starts with humility. It is only when you are willing to go low that God can trust you to go high.

Adding Value First and Trusting God for Provision

One of the greatest secrets of Kingdom wealth is that money follows value. The world chases money, but in the Kingdom, you attract provision by serving, solving problems, and meeting needs. When you focus on adding value to others, wealth comes as a byproduct.

Proverbs 11:25 states, *"The generous soul will be made rich, and he who waters will also be watered himself."* (NKJV)

This means that as you pour into others, you will be poured into. As you give, you will receive. When you make life better for others, God ensures that you are taken care of.

Many people struggle financially because they focus only on what they can receive rather than on what they can give. They ask, *"How can I make more money?"* instead of asking, *"How can I add more value?"* The truth is, the more problems you solve, the more people you serve, and the more lives you impact, the greater your financial increase will be.

Every successful entrepreneur in history became wealthy because they solved a problem. They did not start by chasing riches. They started by meeting a need, creating a solution, or offering something of value that others were willing to pay for. The greatest businesses in the world became successful because they focused on service first.

Jesus modeled this perfectly. He did not come demanding to be honored. He came healing the sick, feeding the hungry, and teaching the lost. His impact was so great that crowds followed Him wherever He went. When you live a life of service, people are drawn to you, opportunities open, and resources flow.

One of the most dangerous misconceptions about leadership is that it means power. The truth is, leadership is not about having authority over people, it is about serving them well.

Jesus made this clear when He said:

"But he who is greatest among you shall be your servant." (Matthew 23:11, NKJV)

The greatest leaders are those who add the most value to others. They do not lead by force but by influence. They do not demand respect; they earn it by their actions. A leader's job is to lift others up, empower them, and make them better.

God promotes those who prioritize the well-being of others. If you want to lead, you must first learn to serve. If you want financial success, you must first become someone who creates value for others.

Walking in the Gift of Entrepreneurship

Entrepreneurship is not just about making money, it is about stewarding a gift. God has given every person talents, abilities, and skills that are designed to serve others. When you walk in these gifts and use them to add value to the world, you are fulfilling your purpose.

Romans 12:6-8 speaks of different gifts given by God, one of them being the gifts of giving with generosity and leading with diligence. Business is a vehicle through which you can express these gifts, whether it is by providing jobs, solving problems, or serving communities.

When you step into entrepreneurship with a heart of service, you are partnering with God's design. You are not just making money, you are fulfilling a Kingdom assignment. You are using your hands, mind, and resources to bless others.

The question is not, *"How can I become wealthy?"* The question is, *"How can I use what God has placed in me to serve others?"* When you answer that question, wealth will follow.

The Coffee Shop That Changed Everything

Daniel had always dreamed of owning his own business. For years, he watched successful entrepreneurs and wondered what set them apart. When he finally opened his own small coffee shop, he was determined to make it profitable. He studied business strategies, watched his competitors, and worked tirelessly to attract customers.

At first, things were slow. People came in occasionally, but there was nothing remarkable about his shop. He struggled to pay his bills, and then doubt began to creep in. One evening, while closing up, he prayed in frustration, *"God, why isn't this working? I've done everything right."*

The next morning, an elderly retired businessman named Mr. Evans came in and sat by the window. As Daniel brought his coffee over, Mr. Evans smiled and asked, "Son, what problem are you solving for people?"

Daniel was taken aback. "I sell coffee," he answered.

Mr. Evans chuckled. "No, you're offering an experience. You're serving people, not just coffee. If you focus on adding value, the money will follow." Those words stuck with Daniel. That night, he read Matthew 20:26 and realized that success in the Kingdom wasn't about how much he could gain but how well he could serve others.

The next day, he changed everything. Instead of just selling coffee, he focused on making every customer's day better. He remembered their names, asked about their families, and created a space where people felt valued. He partnered with local artists, offering them a space to showcase their work. He started a free mentorship night for young entrepreneurs who wanted to learn about business.

Slowly, the shop transformed. Word spread that Daniel's coffee shop wasn't just a place to grab a drink, it was a place where people felt seen, encouraged, and valued. Customers became loyal and new ones poured in. Before he knew it, his struggling shop became the most popular café in town.

One evening, as he locked up, he smiled and whispered, *"Thank You, Lord. I finally understand. It's not about selling, it's about serving."* By adding value to his business, Daniel unlocked the law of Kingdom prosperity. His business flourished not because he chased money, but because he chose to serve others.

Biblical Principles of The Law of Value – Serving Before Selling

1. **True Greatness Comes Through Service** – "Whoever desires to become great among you, let him be your servant." (Matthew 20:26, NKJV)

   o If you desire success, you must first embrace servanthood.

2. **God Rewards Those Who Humble Themselves** – *"And whoever exalts himself will be humbled, and he who humbles himself will be exalted."* (Matthew 23:12, NKJV)

   o True promotion comes through embracing humility, not through self-promotion.

3. **Wealth Follows Value** – *"The generous soul will be made rich, and he who waters will also be watered himself."* (Proverbs 11:25, NKJV)

   o When you add value to others, provision follows.

4. **Leadership is Serving Others** – *"But he who is greatest among you shall be your servant."* (Matthew 23:11, NKJV)

   o True leadership is about gentle influence, not control.

5. **Entrepreneurship is a Gift from God** – *"Having then gifts differing according to the grace that is given to us, let us use them."* (Romans 12:6, NKJV)

   o Business is a tool for fulfilling God's purpose by serving others.

Applying These Principles

- Embrace the heart of a servant. Success begins with servanthood; the more you serve, the greater your impact.

- Walk in humility and let God promote you. True promotion comes from God, not self-exaltation.

- Focus on adding value, not just making sales. When you meet needs and solve problems, provision follows.

- Lead through service, not authority. Leadership is about influence through serving others, not control.

- Use your business as a ministry tool. Your business is a platform for serving others and advancing God's Kingdom.

As an entrepreneur, your business is not just a way to make money; it is a ministry, a vehicle for serving others, and a tool for Kingdom impact. You are not just selling a product or offering a service. You are solving problems, meeting needs, and bringing value to those God has called you to serve. If you have only been focusing on what you can gain, it is time to shift your mindset. Kingdom prosperity is not about chasing money, it is about attracting provision through service. The question is not: *How much can I make*, but rather, *how well can I serve?*

Think about your business or the one you are building. Who are you serving? Are you adding value to your customers, clients, or employees? Are you making people's lives better, easier, or more joyful? Are you approaching each interaction with the heart of a servant, knowing that when you serve well, God ensures you lack nothing?

When you step into this truth, everything changes. You no longer worry about competition because no one can out-serve you. You no longer stress about money because you know provision follows value. You no longer strive to be seen because your service makes you unforgettable. This is how Kingdom entrepreneurs rise, by humbling themselves before God and trusting Him to exalt them in due time. Your breakthrough is waiting on the other side of your service. Your increase is hidden in the value you provide. Your business will flourish when you stop trying to sell and start seeking to serve.

Now is the time to shift your focus. The world tells you to chase success, but the Kingdom calls you to create it, through service, through impact, and through adding value to others. The moment you stop seeking to be served and start serving with excellence, doors will open that no amount of striving could unlock.

You are standing at the threshold of something greater. What you do next will determine your level of increase. Will you continue doing business the world's way, focused on sales, numbers, and transactions? Or will you embrace the divine principle that success is found in how well you serve?

If you are ready for something beyond what you can accomplish in your own strength, the next chapter holds the key for you. The law of multiplication is not just about working harder, it is about God taking what you have and supernaturally increasing it. When you step into this next principle, you will never see business the same way again. Your next level is waiting. Let's go!

6

THE LAW OF MULTIPLICATION
SCALING A BUSINESS GOD'S WAY

God is a God of multiplication. From the beginning of creation, His design for mankind, the earth, and every living thing was to increase and expand. When He blessed Adam and Eve, His first command was, *"Be fruitful and multiply; fill the earth and subdue it"* (Genesis 1:28, NKJV). This was not just about having children; it was a principle of abundance, dominion, and stewardship. Everything in God's Kingdom is designed to grow, and that includes your business, your influence, and your impact.

Yet, many entrepreneurs operate with a mindset of limitation. They work tirelessly, striving in their own strength to create success, only to find themselves exhausted, stuck, or overwhelmed. Multiplication is not just about working harder; it's about working in alignment with Kingdom principles.

When you attempt to build something in your own strength, you will always have to maintain it in your own strength. When you allow God to be the source of your increase, He provides not only the expansion but also the divine wisdom, favor, and strategies to sustain it.

The difference between worldly success and Kingdom multiplication is simple: *Who is your source?* If your source is your own ability, your network, or the economy, then you will constantly live in fear of losing what you have built. However, if your source is God, then no market crash, competition, or economic downturn can stop the increase He has planned for you.

The Responsibility to Multiply

Jesus illustrated the principle of multiplication in the Parable of the Talents:

>*"For the **kingdom of heaven** is like a man traveling to a far country, who called his own servants and delivered his goods to them. And to one he gave five talents, to another two, and to another one, to each according to his own ability; and immediately he went on a journey."* (Matthew 25:14-15, 20-30, NKJV)

In this parable, the master represents God, and the servants represent us. God entrusts each of us with resources: our skills, knowledge, opportunities, relationships, and businesses. What we do with what He gives us determines whether we experience multiplication or stagnation.

- The servant who received five talents doubled what he had and was rewarded.

- The servant who received two talents doubled his as well and was equally rewarded.

- The servant who received one talent did nothing, out of fear he buried it in the ground, and was rebuked by the master and then cast into outer darkness.

The master responded to the first two servants with these powerful words:

>*"Well done, good and faithful servant; you were faithful over a few things, I will make you ruler over many things. Enter into the joy of your lord."* (Matthew 25:21, NKJV)

Multiplication is the result of faithfulness. If you are faithful with what you have now, God will increase it. If you are careless, fearful, or stagnant, you will remain where you are. The servant who buried his talent had the wrong mindset. He was focused on fear, not faith. He saw the master as harsh instead of generous. Many entrepreneurs fail to multiply because they are afraid to step out, afraid to take risks, and afraid to invest in what God has given them. Fear leads to stagnation, but faith leads to expansion. God's expectation is clear! He does not want us to maintain; He wants us to multiply.

Wealth is Created by Serving More People

In the previous chapter, we uncovered a powerful Kingdom principle, wealth follows service. We explored how true success does not come from chasing money but from adding value to others. Now, we will take that understanding deeper by examining how serving more people is the key to multiplication.

Many entrepreneurs believe that in order to make more money, they need to charge higher prices, expand their offerings, or work harder. While these strategies have their place, the simplest and most sustainable way to increase wealth is by serving more people. Every great business, whether small or large, thrives because it meets a need on a greater scale. The more people you impact, the greater your increase.

Jesus modeled this principle in His ministry. He never focused on accumulating wealth, yet His influence grew exponentially because He continually served the multitudes. He fed five thousand with five loaves and two fish (Matthew 14:17-21). He healed all who came to Him (Matthew 8:16). He taught crowds that stretched beyond what the disciples could count. His focus was never self-promotion, yet His name is the most well known in history.

If you want your business to grow, the key question is not, *how can I make more money?* but rather, *how can I serve more people effectively?*

The Power of Scaling Service

A business that serves ten people has a limited impact. A business that serves a thousand people increases its revenue, reach, and influence.

Scaling is not just about working harder, it is about increasing your capacity to help others.

The fastest-growing businesses in the world all operate on this principle. They don't just solve problems; they solve them for millions. A company that provides shoes for ten people will never reach the level of a company that provides shoes for ten thousand. A coach who mentors five clients will never see the same impact as one who trains five hundred.

For Kingdom entrepreneurs, this is not just a business strategy, it is a divine assignment. God blesses those who make it their mission to serve His people well. Proverbs 11:25 declares, *"The generous soul will be made rich, and he who waters will also be watered himself."* (NKJV). If you dedicate yourself to pouring into others, God ensures that you are also filled.

Multiplication Happens Through Systems and Structure

One of the biggest mistakes entrepreneurs make is trying to do everything themselves. A business that relies entirely upon one person cannot multiply. If you are the only one delivering the service, making the decisions, or interacting with customers, your growth will always be limited by your personal capacity.

To truly scale your impact, you must create systems that allow you to serve more people without sacrificing quality. Jesus Himself demonstrated this when He sent out the seventy disciples to minister (Luke 10:1). He did not try to do everything alone, rather He empowered others to carry the work forward.

This means building a structure that allows for growth. Whether it is through hiring a team, developing automation, or creating repeatable processes, the goal is to serve more people without burning yourself out. The best leaders do not just lead, they equip others to lead, ensuring that their influence and impact continue to multiply.

The More You Serve, the More You Receive

Luke 6:38 lays out a simple but profound truth: *"Give, and it will be given to you: good measure, pressed down, shaken together, and running over will be put into your bosom."* (NKJV).

This principle applies not only to finances but to business. The more value you give, the more opportunity, influence, and provision will come your way. Entrepreneurs who are obsessed with making money often struggle because they focus on getting rather than giving. Those who focus on serving others find that wealth begins to follow them effortlessly.

When you understand this, you stop chasing success and start attracting it. You stop seeing business as a transaction and start seeing it as an assignment. I once heard a very wise man say, "You realize that money is simply a reflection of how many people you have helped."

Expanding Your Impact Starts Now

If you are serious about multiplication, ask yourself:

- How can I structure my business to serve more people?

- What systems can I put in place to expand my reach?

- Who can I empower to help carry the vision forward?

- How can I ensure that my service remains excellent even as I scale?

These questions will determine whether you remain at your current level or step into supernatural increase. Multiplication is not reserved for the privileged, it is promised to those who steward what they have well and are willing to serve at a greater level. What you do next will determine your level of growth. Will you stay small, or will you expand your capacity to serve more people and trust God for the increase?

The Best Leaders Empower Others to Lead

Another key to multiplication is learning to delegate and develop others as leaders. Many entrepreneurs limit themselves because they try to do everything on their own. They hesitate to trust others, fearing that no one can do the job as well as they can. This mindset creates bottlenecks in business and keeps growth stagnant.

Moses faced this issue when leading Israel. He tried to handle every dispute and decision alone until his father-in-law, Jethro, gave him wise counsel:

"Both you and these people who are with you will surely wear yourselves out. For this thing is too much for you; you are not able to perform it by yourself." (Exodus 18:18, NKJV)

Jethro advised Moses to appoint capable leaders to help carry the load, freeing him to focus on what only he could do. The result was a nation that functioned more effectively and leadership that multiplied. The best leaders are not those who hold on to power but those who empower others to lead.

Jesus Himself demonstrated this principle. He did not try to do everything alone, rather He trained His disciples to continue the work after He ascended. He gave them authority, equipped them, and sent them out. Multiplication happens when leaders raise up other leaders.

If you want your business to scale, you must:

1. **Train and mentor others** – Teach those around you to operate in excellence and with integrity.

2. **Delegate wisely** – Focus on what only you can do and entrust others with responsibilities which can be delegated.

3. **Build a leadership culture** – Equip people to think and operate at a higher level than as mere entry level employees.

A business that relies solely on one person will never multiply. A business that raises up leaders will grow beyond limits.

A Single Mother's Journey in Business

Kim had every reason to doubt. As a single mother of two young children, stepping into entrepreneurship felt like an impossible dream. She had no financial cushion, no wealthy investors, and no guarantee that her business would succeed. What she did have was a deep conviction that God had called her to something greater, and an unshakable belief that if she served well, He would take care of the rest.

Her business was simple; consulting and training for small businesses looking to improve their operations. She had the skills, the passion, and the heart to help others, but she had no clients. No one knew her name, and she had no money for expensive marketing campaigns. Instead of focusing on what she lacked, she leaned into what she could give. Rather than worrying about making sales, she decided to serve.

She reached out to local business owners, offering free workshops to train their teams. She gave away strategies and resources without asking for anything in return. Some people told her she was crazy. "You need to charge for that!" they insisted. Kim wasn't focused on immediate profit. She was focused on adding value first and trusting God to multiply her efforts.

Days turned into weeks, and though she was working tirelessly, she still saw no financial return. The bills piled up, and fear knocked at her door. Still, she chose faith over fear. She clung to Galatians 6:9 which instructs us, *"And let us not grow weary while doing good, for in due season we shall reap if we do not lose heart."* (NKJV).

She refused to stop serving, even when her situation looked bleak. She prayed over every business she helped, asking God to bless them even before He blessed her. She continued to give her time, her skills, and her expertise, sowing into others while trusting that her harvest was on its way. Then, finally the breakthrough came.

One of the businesses she had served for free saw dramatic improvements in their operations. The owner was so grateful that he referred her to another company, this time, a paying client. That client referred her to three more. Within months, the demand for her services exploded! People sought her out, not because of flashy advertisements, but because of the undeniable impact she had made.

Soon, she was able to set her prices, hire a small team, and expand her reach. Her business flourished, not because she chased money, but because she freely offered service. Every seed she had sown into others returned to her, multiplied beyond what she imagined.

One evening, as she put her children to bed, she knelt beside them and whispered a prayer of gratitude: *"Lord, You are faithful. You did it Your way, not mine."*

Kim had stepped into the law of multiplication. She had trusted God's Kingdom principles instead of the world's methods. She had given when she had nothing, and God had multiplied her faith into an abundant harvest. Her story was no longer just about business, it was a testimony of what happens when you serve first, trust fully, and refuse to give up. She had not just built a business; she had built a legacy!

Biblical Principles of The Law of Multiplication

1. **Faithfulness leads to increase** – *"You were faithful over a few things, I will make you ruler over many things."* (Matthew 25:21, NKJV)

   o When you manage what God has given you well, He will multiply it.

2. **Fear prevents multiplication** – *"And I was afraid, and went and hid your talent in the ground."* (Matthew 25:25, NKJV)

   o Those who fear taking action will remain stagnant.

3. **Wealth follows service** – *"Give, and it will be given to you."* (Luke 6:38, NKJV)

    o The more people you serve, the greater your impact and financial increase.

4. **Empowering others multiplies success** – *"Both you and these people who are with you will surely wear yourselves out."* (Exodus 18:18, NKJV)

    o To scale your business, you must develop and empower others.

Applying These Principles

- Faithfulness leads to increase. Steward what you have with excellence, and God will trust you with more.

- Fear prevents multiplication. Refusing to act out of fear will keep you stuck and unfruitful.

- Wealth follows service. The more value you bring to others, the more increase flows back to you.

- Empowering others multiplies success. Raising up others to lead will expand your capacity and influence.

Scaling your business God's way is not about exhausting yourself with more effort. It is about stepping into alignment with His divine principles. Multiplication is not a product of striving; it is a byproduct of faithfulness. When you steward what you have been given well, serve others with excellence, and empower others to succeed as leaders, expansion becomes inevitable. What you hold in your hands right now is only the beginning. God is a God of increase, and when you trust Him as your source rather than relying on your own strength, He brings supernatural multiplication that far exceeds human effort. The harvest is always greater than the seed, but only when the seed is sown.

Now is the time to step boldly into this truth. Will you continue to rely on your own strength, or will you embrace the law of multiplication and watch God do what only He can? The next chapter takes this concept to a new level that isn't just about what you yourself accomplish, it's about who you lead. Get ready to step into leadership that transforms lives and leaves an impact far beyond mere monetary profit for yourself. Let's move forward.

Part 3

LEADERSHIP & INFLUENCE

Leadership is more than a title. It is more than authority, position, or recognition. True leadership, the kind that transforms lives and leaves a lasting impact, is about serving, empowering, and influencing others for the glory of God.

The world often defines leadership as power, control, and dominance over others. It teaches that only the strongest, loudest, and most ruthless rise to the top. Yet, in the Kingdom of God, leadership is the opposite. True leaders do not seek to be served, they choose to serve. They do not demand loyalty, they inspire it. They do not chase greatness, they humble themselves, and God lifts them up.

Jesus, the greatest leader of all time, modeled this perfectly. He led with love, wisdom, and unwavering purpose. He influenced nations without force, guided His disciples with patience, and changed the course of history by laying down His own life for others. His leadership was not about self-promotion, but about empowering others to step into their divine calling.

This section will challenge everything the world has taught you about leadership. You will learn:

- **How to lead in a way that glorifies God**—with integrity, wisdom, and faith.

- **The power of influence**—why leadership is not about control, but rather about impact.

- **How to empower others to lead**—because multiplication doesn't happen when you do everything yourself; it happens when you equip others to rise.

If you desire to scale your business, expand your reach, and build something that lasts, you must learn to lead God's way. Influence is not just about what you achieve; it's about what you leave behind. Are you ready to lead at a level that brings transformation? The principles in this section will elevate not just your business, but your life. Let's dive in.

7

LEADERSHIP THAT GLORIFIES GOD

Leadership in the Kingdom of God is radically different from leadership within the world. While the world defines leadership as power, control, and dominance, Kingdom leadership is about servanthood, humility, and influence. The world elevates those who command and demand, while God exalts those who serve and empower.

Jesus Himself gave the clearest definition of true leadership when He told His disciples:

"Yet it shall not be so among you; but whoever desires to become great among you, let him be your servant. And whoever desires to be first among you, let him be your slave—just as the Son of Man did not come to be served, but to serve, and to give His life a ransom for many." (Matthew 20:26-28, NKJV)

Servant Leadership vs. Authoritarian Leadership

Worldly leadership is about position. It is built on hierarchy, where those at the top control and command those beneath them. It often relies upon fear, manipulation, or coercion to maintain authority. Many leaders today seek personal gain, valuing power over people. Their focus is on how many serve them, rather than how they can serve others.

Kingdom leadership is about responsibility. It is built on humility, where leaders recognize that their authority is given by God to serve, uplift, and develop others. True leaders do not see people as tools for their own success; they see people as their assignment for service. They lead not through control but through influence, wisdom, and love.

Jesus, the ultimate leader, demonstrated this in everything He did. He had all power and authority, yet He washed the feet of His disciples (John 13:12-15). He could have demanded service, yet He chose to serve. He led by example. He did not lord His authority over others, He invited them into transformation through love and truth.

Paul reinforced this principle when he wrote:

"Let nothing be done through selfish ambition or conceit, but in lowliness of mind let each esteem others better than himself. Let each of you look out not only for his own interests, but also for the interests of others." (Philippians 2:3-4, NKJV)

This is the difference: The world's leaders seek to be served. God's leaders seek to serve others.

One of my favorite leaders, John C. Maxwell states, *"Leadership is influence—nothing more, nothing less."* True leadership is not about a title; it is about the ability to impact and inspire others. A person does not need a position to be a leader, they need character, vision, and a heart to serve.

The Bible consistently shows us that leadership is not determined by status but by influence and faithfulness.

- **Joseph** had no official title in Potiphar's house, yet he became the most trusted man in his master's household because of his integrity and wisdom (Genesis 39:2-6).

- **Daniel** had no claim to leadership in Babylon, yet his excellence and devotion to God positioned him to influence kings (Daniel 6).

- **David** was an unknown shepherd boy, yet his heart for God made him the greatest king Israel ever had (1 Samuel 16:7).

People do not follow leaders because of their title, they follow them because of who they are. Influence is earned through trust, wisdom, and service. Those who lead like Jesus will naturally attract others, not through force, but through the undeniable impact of their lives.

Jesus' influence was so strong that people left everything to follow Him. He never manipulated, never forced, never coerced, yet thousands followed Him because His leadership gave life, purpose, and transformation to their lives.

Becoming a Leader Worth Following

Another one of my favorite leaders, Craig Groeschel teaches that *"People would rather follow a leader who is real than a leader who is always right."* Many leaders today chase perfection, trying to appear flawless and always in control. Kingdom leaders, however, lead from authenticity, humility, and a dependence on God.

A leader worth following is:

1. **Humble, not prideful** – *"God resists the proud, but gives grace to the humble."* (James 4:6, NKJV)

    o Arrogance repels people as well as God; humility draws them in.

2. **Trustworthy, not deceitful** – *"Moreover it is required in stewards that one be found faithful."* (1 Corinthians 4:2, NKJV)

    o A leader who cannot be trusted will eventually lose their influence.

3. **Focused on people, not power** – *"Shepherd the flock of God which is among you, serving as overseers, not by compulsion but willingly, not for dishonest gain but eagerly."* (1 Peter 5:2, NKJV)

    o A leader's primary role is to develop others, not use them.

4. **Secure, not threatened by others' success** – *"A man's gift makes room for him, and brings him before great men."* (Romans 12:15, NKJV)

   o A strong leader celebrates the success of others and raises others up.

5. **A servant, not a dictator** – *"But he who is greatest among you shall be your servant."* (Matthew 23:11, NKJV)

   o A true leader leads by serving first.

Kingdom Leadership vs. Worldly Leadership Today

Look at the world's leadership today. Many people in authority demand recognition, yet their character does not merit respect. They make promises but lack integrity. They seek power but fail to serve. They desire followers, but few truly follow them from the heart.

Now compare this to how Jesus led. He didn't demand a throne; He carried a cross. He didn't rule with fear; He led with love. He didn't seek followers; He called disciples. Kingdom leadership is not about how many serve you, but how many you serve. It is not about building your own name; it is about building God's Kingdom. It is not about commanding; it is about influencing through wisdom, love, and truth.

The Leadership That Built or Broke a Business

Ethan and Paul both launched tech startups in the same year and in the same city, with nearly identical funding. They both had groundbreaking ideas, talented teams, and a hunger for success. Yet, the way they led their companies would determine their fate.

One would build a lasting legacy, while the other would watch everything fall apart.

Paul: The Worldly CEO

Paul had one goal: to dominate the market and build an empire. From day one, he made it clear that his company was about winning at all costs. His leadership was built on authority, fear, and self-interest. He micromanaged everything, believing that no one could do the job as well as he could. He expected his employees to work around the clock, pushing them to their limits with little regard for their well-being. Promotions were rare, and when they did happen, they were based on favoritism, not merit.

When making business deals, Paul focused solely on profit margins and power. He cut corners, overpromised to clients, and underpaid his employees. He convinced himself that this was how leadership worked: "if you don't control people, they'll walk all over you." Paul thrived in the short term. Investors were impressed by the company's aggressive growth. Profits soared. Employees tolerated the toxic culture because of the pay. Meanwhile, beneath the surface, everything was unraveling.

Employees were exhausted and resentful. The company's reputation took a hit as clients started noticing the lack of integrity in James' leadership. Innovation stalled because no one felt safe sharing new ideas. People feared making mistakes more than they wanted to succeed.

The Bible warns against this kind of leadership:

"A ruler who lacks understanding is a great oppressor, but he who hates covetousness will prolong his days." (Proverbs 28:16, NKJV)

Paul had built a business, but he had not built trust, loyalty, or influence by seeking to understand the needs and desires of his employees.

Ethan: The Kingdom CEO

Ethan had a different approach. He didn't just want to build a company, he wanted to build people, relationships, and a culture that glorified God. His leadership model was based on serving others first. From day one, he made it clear that his business was not just about making money, it was about solving problems, adding value, and serving both his customers and his employees well. Ethan followed Jesus' model of leadership:

"But he who is greatest among you shall be your servant." (Matthew 23:11, NKJV)

He treated his employees with dignity, creating an environment where they felt valued, heard, and empowered. Instead of micromanaging, Ethan delegated, trusted, and developed leaders within his team. He held regular meetings where employees could voice their ideas without fear. Instead of just demanding results, he invested in the growth of his people.

Rather than chasing quick profits, Ethan focused on building trust and delivering value. He paid his employees fairly, ensured ethical business practices, and put people before profits. He sought wisdom from God in every major decision, refusing to compromise integrity for financial gain.

"The generous soul will be made rich, and he who waters will also be watered himself." (Proverbs 11:25, NKJV)

Ethan's company grew steadily, not because he forced it to, but because he built a culture of trust, collaboration, and service. Employees loved working there, and their passion fueled innovation. Clients became loyal because they knew they were working with a company that stood for something more than money. Investors took notice, not just of the numbers, but of the long-term vision. Ethan understood that true leadership is influence. He didn't demand respect;

he earned it. He didn't control his employees; he empowered them. He didn't chase wealth; he served people, and wealth followed.

Two Leaders, Two Outcomes

After five years, the difference was undeniable. Pauls' company collapsed under its own weight. Key employees left, taking their knowledge and expertise with them. His investors pulled out when they saw the company's declining morale and reputation. The once-thriving business crumbled because it had been built on fear, greed, and control.

However, Ethan's company thrived and expanded. His employees were deeply invested in the mission. His clients spread the word, growing the business without the need for aggressive sales tactics. He didn't just build a successful company, he built a lasting legacy of integrity, service, and Kingdom impact.

Pauls' leadership had power, but no influence so it died and went nowhere.

Ethan's leadership had influence, and God multiplied it, making it a lasting legacy.

Leadership is not about how many people work for you; it's about how many people you serve. The world teaches that leadership is about control, dominance, and personal gain. God's Kingdom teaches that true leadership is about humility, servanthood, and empowering others.

"Whoever desires to become great among you, let him be your servant. And whoever desires to be first among you, let him be your slave—just as the Son of Man did not come to be served, but to serve, and to give His life a ransom for many." (Matthew 20:26-28, NKJV)

If you want to lead in a way that glorifies God, ask yourself:

- Am I leading with service or control?

- Do I inspire loyalty, or do I enforce compliance?

- Am I building people, or just building profits?

- Do I empower others to lead, or do I hoard all the power?

The greatest leaders are not the ones with the most authority, but the ones with the most influence. True influence comes from a heart that serves.

Which kind of leader will you choose to be?

Biblical Principles of Leadership That Glorifies God

1. **The greatest leader is the greatest servant** – *"Whoever desires to become great among you, let him be your servant."* (Matthew 20:26, NKJV)

   o Leadership is about lifting others through service, not ruling over them.

2. **Leadership is about influence, not position** – *"A man's gift makes room for him, and brings him before great men."* (Proverbs 18:16, NKJV)

   o You don't need a title to lead, you need wisdom, integrity, and service.

3. **Humility leads to promotion** – *"Humble yourselves in the sight of the Lord, and He will lift you up."* (James 4:10, NKJV)

   o God promotes those who serve with humility.

4. **True leaders develop others** – *"And the things that you have heard from me among many witnesses, commit these to faithful men who will be able to teach others also."* (2 Timothy 2:2, NKJV)

   o Leadership is about raising up more leaders.

5. **Godly leadership brings honor and stability** – *"When the righteous are in authority, the people rejoice; but when a wicked man rules, the people groan."* (Proverbs 29:2, NKJV)

o The world needs righteous leaders who lead with integrity.

Applying These Principles:

- Lead through service, not status. Choose to serve others first, reflecting the heart of Christ in all you do.

- Influence is greater than a title. Let your integrity and example speak louder than any position.

- Walk in humility, and let God do the elevating. Stay low before God, and He will lift you up in His perfect timing.

- Develop people, not just profits. Invest in others by equipping and empowering them to grow and lead.

- Lead with righteousness and integrity. Build a foundation of trust by doing what is right, even when it costs.

Whether you recognize it or not, your leadership is influencing those around you, your employees, your clients, your family, and even those who simply observe how you carry yourself. Leadership is not about position; it is about impact. Every decision you make, every conversation you have, and every action you take is shaping the kind of leader you are becoming.

The question is, are you leading in a way that glorifies God? Are you inspiring, serving, and empowering others? Or are you leading the way the world does, focused on control, recognition, and self-preservation?

Great leaders are not remembered for how much power they held, but for how many lives they transformed. Your leadership is either building something that will last or something that will fade away. In the next chapter, we will go deeper into what it means to lead with excellence, integrity, and wisdom. Because leadership is not just about today, it's about creating an impact that lasts for generations. If you are ready to become the kind of leader people don't just follow but a leader they are inspired by, keep reading. Let's take this journey to another level.

8

INTEGRITY & EXCELLENCE IN BUSINESS

Integrity and excellence are not optional in the Kingdom of God, they are foundational. A business that lacks integrity may succeed for a season, but it will never experience lasting prosperity. A leader who does not operate with a spirit of excellence may gain influence temporarily, but over time, their character will determine their legacy.

The Bible makes this clear in Proverbs 11:3 where it states:

"The integrity of the upright will guide them, but the perversity of the unfaithful will destroy them." (NKJV)

This verse speaks directly to the way we conduct business, make decisions, and lead others. Integrity is not just about honesty, it is about living in alignment with God's principles. Those who walk in integrity will be guided by wisdom, peace, and divine favor, while those who choose deception and compromise will ultimately be undone by their own actions.

What Does Proverbs 11:3 Really Mean?

This verse presents a powerful contrast between two types of people:

1. **The upright—those who walk in integrity.** These individuals make decisions based upon righteousness, truth, and honor. Their path is clear because they do not have to hide anything or fear exposure. Integrity becomes their guide, ensuring they stay on a course that leads to lasting prosperity.

2. **The unfaithful—those who engage in deception and dishonesty.** Their choices are driven by greed, selfish ambition, or the desire to take shortcuts. Eventually, their lack of integrity will bring destruction, whether through loss of reputation, broken trust, or divine judgment.

In business, this principle plays out every day. Entrepreneurs who build their companies on truth, fairness, and ethical practices will experience stability and divine direction. Those who cut corners, manipulate, or chase success at any cost may experience temporary gains, but the weight of their dishonesty will eventually catch up to them. The world often rewards compromise, encouraging people to do whatever it takes to get ahead. The Kingdom of God operates differently. God does not just bless effort, He blesses righteousness.

Many people assume that success is measured by wealth alone. If someone has money, power, and influence, the world calls them successful. Yet, wealth gained without integrity is not true prosperity, it is spiritual poverty. When financial gain comes at the cost of honesty, fairness, and godly principles, it does not bring peace, it brings anxiety. It does not create security, it invites collapse.

The Bible warns of this in Proverbs 13:11,

"Wealth gained by dishonesty will be diminished, but he who gathers by labor will increase." (NKJV)

Dishonestly achieved wealth never lasts. Businesses that manipulate customers, exploit workers, or engage in unethical practices may thrive for a while, but eventually, their corruption catches up with them. Whether through legal consequences, loss of reputation, or personal downfall, money that is obtained without integrity eventually vanishes.

True prosperity is built on trust, righteousness, and long-term faithfulness. God desires His people to prosper, but not through compromise. He blesses those who honor Him in their work, who serve others with integrity, and who remain faithful even when no one is watching.

Integrity Is the Foundation of Trust

Trust is the currency of every successful business and leadership role. People do not follow leaders they cannot trust. Customers do not remain loyal to businesses that deceive them. Employees will not give their best to a company that does not honor its word. Integrity is the foundation that makes everything else work. Without it, businesses crumble, leadership fails, and relationships break.

Proverbs 22:1 emphasizes this truth:

"A good name is to be chosen rather than great riches, loving favor rather than silver and gold." (NKJV)

A business with integrity may not always experience the fastest growth, but it will experience the most sustainable growth. A leader with integrity may not always rise the quickest, but they will remain standing the longest. Trust is not built in a day, but it can be destroyed in an instant. Integrity must be non-negotiable in every aspect of business.

The Excellence Factor, Why It Sets You Apart

Integrity ensures that what you build will last, but excellence determines the level of impact you will have. God calls His people to a higher standard in everything they do. Mediocrity does not reflect His nature. He is a God of order, wisdom, and excellence.

Colossians 3:23 commands:

"And whatever you do, do it heartily, as to the Lord and not to men." (NKJV)

This means that every action, every product, every service, and every decision should be done with excellence, as an offering to God.

Businesses that operate with excellence:

- Pay attention to details and produce high-quality work.

- Serve customers with care and diligence.

- Constantly seek growth, improvement, and innovation.

- Lead employees with honor, wisdom, and respect.

Excellence is not about perfection, it is about consistency and intentionality. Those who commit to excellence attract opportunities, customers, and divine favor.

Proverbs 22:29 reinforces this:

"Do you see a man who excels in his work? He will stand before kings; he will not stand before unknown men." (NKJV)

Excellence elevates people to places of influence. Those who commit to going above and beyond will always be in demand.

A Business Built to Last

Logan had always dreamed of running his own construction business. After years of working under different contractors, he had seen both the right way and the wrong way to build a company. Some business owners cut corners, used subpar materials, and overcharged clients while delivering mediocre work. Others were obsessed with perfection, constantly delaying projects because nothing ever seemed "good enough." Logan knew there had to be a better way. A way that honored both people and God.

When he finally launched his own company, True Foundations Construction, he made a commitment: every project would be built with integrity, and every job would be done with excellence.

His business took off quickly. Word spread that Logan's company was different, he didn't rush jobs just to move on to the next paycheck, and he refused to deceive customers with hidden costs or cheap materials. Contractors and competitors took notice, and not all of them were pleased.

One day, a high-profile developer approached Logan with a massive contract that could triple his company's revenue. It was the kind of deal that could put True Foundations Construction on the map. The only problem? The developer wanted Logan to use cheaper materials while charging the client for high-quality ones.

"Everyone does it," the developer said with a smirk. "They'll never know the difference. It's just business."

Logan felt the weight of the decision. If he agreed, he'd make more money in a single deal than he had in the past two years. His employees would get bigger bonuses, his company could expand, and he could finally upgrade his equipment.

Still, something inside him hesitated. He remembered Proverbs 11:3,

"The integrity of the upright will guide them, but the perversity of the unfaithful will destroy them." (NKJV)

Logan had built his business on honesty, and he knew that the moment he compromised, everything he had worked for would lose its foundation. "I appreciate the opportunity," Logan said, looking the developer in the eye, "but I don't do business that way. I build with integrity, and that means delivering what I promise, no exceptions."

The developer scoffed. "Suit yourself. There are plenty of other companies who will take this deal." Logan walked away, knowing he had just turned down a life-changing contract. Doubt crept in, had he made a mistake? Could he afford to keep running his business without shortcuts?

Weeks later, his phone rang. A new client had heard about Logan's commitment to quality and integrity. He owned multiple properties and was looking for a contractor he could trust for long-term projects, a contract twice the size of the one Logan had just turned down.

Integrity had guided him, and God had multiplied his faithfulness.

Logan's company continued to grow, not just because of his integrity, but because of his commitment to excellence. Unlike perfectionists, who delay projects and refuse to launch anything unless it's flawless, Logan understood that excellence was about giving his best with what he had, not about obsessing over unrealistic standards.

Logan trained his employees to take pride in their work without fear of failure. If mistakes happened, they corrected them and moved forward, rather than being paralyzed by the pursuit of perfection. His company became known for delivering high-quality work on time and with integrity.

Proverbs 22:29 proved true in his life:

"Do you see a man who excels in his work? He will stand before kings; he will not stand before unknown men." (NKJV)

Over time, True Foundations Construction became one of the most trusted firms in the region. Not because Logan had the most money, the most employees, or the flashiest marketing, but because he built his business on integrity and excellence.

Integrity is not just about telling the truth, it's about living in a way that honors God in every decision. Excellence is not about being perfect, it's about consistently delivering your best. Entrepreneurs who embrace these principles will build businesses that not only succeed financially, but leave a legacy of trust, impact, and Kingdom influence.

The question is, what kind of foundation are you building your business upon? Compromise may bring temporary success, but integrity and excellence create prosperity that lasts.

Choose well. The future of your business depends on it.

Biblical Principles of Integrity & Excellence in Business

1. **Integrity leads to stability and divine guidance.** – *"The integrity of the upright will guide them, but the perversity of the unfaithful will destroy them."* (Proverbs 11:3, NKJV)

    o Righteous decisions bring clarity, wisdom, and sustainability.

2. **Wealth gained without integrity will not last.** – *"Wealth gained by dishonesty will be diminished, but he who gathers by labor will increase."* (Proverbs 13:11, NKJV)

    o Finances without integrity lead to loss, anxiety, and destruction.

3. **A good name is worth more than riches.** – *"A good name is to be chosen rather than great riches, loving favor rather than silver and gold."* (Proverbs 22:1, NKJV)

    o Trust and reputation are priceless assets in leadership.

4. **Excellence opens doors to greater influence.** – *"Do you see a man who excels in his work? He will stand before kings; he will not stand before unknown men."* (Proverbs 22:29, NKJV)

    o Those who pursue excellence will be recognized and promoted.

5. **Everything should be done with excellence for God.** – *"And whatever you do, do it heartily, as to the Lord and not to men."* (Colossians 3:23, NKJV)

    o Excellence is not for human approval but for Kingdom impact.

Applying These Principles:

- Integrity leads to stability and divine guidance. Make righteous decisions that align with God's wisdom for long-term success.

- Wealth gained without integrity will not last. Build your business honestly, knowing that shortcuts lead to instability.

- A good name is worth more than riches. Prioritize trust, credibility, and reputation over financial gain.

- Excellence opens doors to greater influence. Commit to high standards in your work, and watch God elevate you.

- Everything should be done with excellence for God – Work with diligence and purpose, knowing you are ultimately serving the Lord.

The way you conduct business and lead others is a direct reflection of your faith. If integrity is compromised, your foundation is weak. If excellence is ignored, your influence is limited. God is calling you to build something that lasts, not just in this life, but for eternity.

Are you leading with integrity? Are you pursuing excellence in everything you do? The world may settle for shortcuts and compromise, but in the Kingdom, success is built on character, consistency, and commitment to righteousness.

The next chapter will take this even further, revealing how to establish a Kingdom-driven business culture that shapes industries, transforms communities, and honors God. If you are ready to create a business that not only prospers but leaves a legacy of righteousness, keep reading. This is where true impact begins.

9

FAITHFUL FINANCES
BIBLICAL MONEY MANAGEMENT

Money is not evil. Money is a tool. How we handle it determines whether it is a blessing or a burden, a resource for impact or a stumbling block leading to destruction. Many believers struggle financially, not because God has not provided, but because they have not been faithful stewards of what He has already placed in their hands. Faithfulness in finances is about aligning money with God's principles; not just acquiring wealth, but managing it in a way that honors Him.

The world operates on a financial system built on debt, greed, and short-term gains. Society teaches that accumulating wealth is the goal, that debt is necessary for success, and that saving money without purpose is the safest way to prepare for the future. However, God's financial system is entirely different. He calls us to steward, multiply, and trust Him, not to hoard, manipulate, or chase wealth blindly.

The Bondage of Debt

"The rich rules over the poor, and the borrower is servant to the lender." (Proverbs 22:7, NKJV)

Debt is one of the greatest financial traps preventing believers from experiencing true financial freedom. The world encourages borrowing as a normal part of life, whether for homes, cars, business ventures, or even vacations. Many believe that debt is necessary for success, but the Bible warns that borrowing actually creates bondage. When someone is in debt, they are not fully free. Their financial decisions are controlled by lenders, payments, and interest rates, instead of being led by the Spirit of God. Debt can limit a person's ability to give, invest, and pursue new opportunities. A person enslaved to debt is not free to fully obey God's financial instructions because they are constantly working to pay off past obligations.

While some forms of debt, such as business loans or real estate investments, can be used strategically, many people take on unnecessary debt for instant gratification, not operating in divine wisdom. Instead of financing unnecessary purchases, believers must learn to steward what they have, multiply wisely, and trust God for increase. God's ultimate desire is for His people to be lenders, not borrowers:

"You shall lend to many nations, but you shall not borrow; you shall reign over many nations, but they shall not reign over you." (Deuteronomy 15:6, NKJV)

Avoiding unnecessary debt and making wise financial choices positions believers to experience true freedom and be able to live with a spirit of generosity.

Trusting God with What You Have

Many people believe they do not have enough to get out of debt, start a business, or give generously. They assume that increase comes from external sources rather than recognizing the full value of what God has already placed in their hands.

The widow in 2 Kings 4:1-7 is a powerful example of how God provides through what we already have, even when we don't realize its value. She was in a desperate financial situation. Her husband had died, and creditors were coming to take her two sons as slaves to pay off her debts. She saw lack, but God saw provision. She cried out to the prophet Elisha, and his response was simple:

"What shall I do for you? Tell me, what do you have in the house?" (2 Kings 4:2, NKJV)

At first, she thought she had nothing. Then she remembered: a small jar of oil. Elisha instructed her to borrow empty vessels from her neighbors and begin pouring the oil. As she obeyed, the oil multiplied. She kept pouring until every vessel was full. Then Elisha gave her the final instruction:

"Go, sell the oil and pay your debt; and you and your sons live on the rest." (2 Kings 4:7, NKJV)

This story reveals several key financial principles:

1. Provision is already in our possession – The widow thought she had nothing, but God had already given her a resource that could be multiplied.

2. Obedience unlocks multiplication – The oil didn't multiply until she acted in faith. Many believers are waiting for God to bless them, while God is waiting for them to move in faith with what they have.

3. Debt should be paid off, not carried forever – Elisha instructed her to sell the oil, pay her debts, and live off the rest. God's plan was for her to be debt-free and have more than enough.

Many today are like the widow, crying out for financial breakthrough while overlooking what God has already given them. Faithfulness in finances begins with recognizing what is in your hand and trusting God to multiply it. Remember also that Jesus first thanked the Father for what He had at hand and then the Father multiplied it (Matthew 14:17-21).

The Love of Money

"For the love of money is a root of all kinds of evil, for which some have strayed from the faith in their greediness, and pierced themselves through with many sorrows." (1 Timothy 6:10, NKJV)

This verse is often misunderstood. Money itself is not evil, the love of money is.

Loving money means:

- Trusting wealth more than trusting God.

- Pursuing money at the expense of character and relationships.

- Making financial decisions based on fear or greed instead of faith.

Some people believe that having money makes them successful. Others believe that having no money makes them holy. Both are wrong. Money is neutral, it takes on the character of the person who holds it. God blesses His people financially so that they can be a blessing to others. If money is controlled by a righteous heart, it will be used for Kingdom purposes. If money is controlled by a greedy heart, it will lead to destruction. A person who loves money will compromise, manipulate, or neglect their faith to get it. But a person who loves God more than money will use finances to serve and advance His will.

Money is a Tool for Impact

Money is meant to create impact, not just comfort. When wealth is placed in the hands of a righteous person, it becomes a powerful tool for transformation. It can fund ministries, provide for families, create opportunities for others, and expand businesses that honor God. Money is not the goal; it is a resource that allows individuals to serve and bring change to those around them.

Proverbs 19:17 states, *"He who has pity on the poor lends to the LORD, and He will pay back what he has given."* (NKJV). This reveals that money, when used correctly, is not just about accumulation, it is about stewardship and following God's plan when we use it. The way we use finances is a direct reflection of our priorities. A person who hoards wealth for self-indulgence misses the greater purpose of money, while someone who uses their resources to bless others aligns with God's heart for provision.

The world often teaches that money is a measure of power or status, but in reality, the amount of money a person has often reflects the value they have provided to others. Those who solve problems, bring innovation, and serve other people well tend to attract more financial resources. This is a Kingdom principle, when you give value, you receive increase. A business that helps thousands of people will naturally have greater financial flow than one that only serves a few. Financial success is not just about working harder; it is about serving better.

God does not bless people with wealth just for their own personal gain. He entrusts it to those who understand that money is a vehicle for advancing His Kingdom purposes on the earth. The world sees money as something to hoard, flaunt, or control, but God sees money as a resource to build, bless, and expand His Kingdom. Those who align with this mindset will not only experience financial freedom but will also walk in the divine responsibility of using wealth to make a lasting impact.

Money Follows Discipline, Not Desire

Many people dream of financial success, yet very few experience it at the level which they desire. The difference is not simply a matter of luck or opportunity, it is a matter of discipline. Proverbs 21:5 (NKJV) states, *"The plans of the diligent lead surely to plenty, but those of everyone who is hasty, surely to poverty."* This verse emphasizes that success is a direct result of diligence and careful planning. Those who take the time to plan, strategize, and execute consistently will eventually see the fruit of their labor. On the other hand, those who seek quick results without discipline or patience often find themselves in financial hardship.

Many people operate with a mindset of urgency, hoping to get rich overnight by jumping right into high-risk investments, or spending impulsively without thinking of long-term consequences. The world markets instant gratification; buy now, pay later; invest fast, profit big; enjoy today, worry tomorrow. However, Scripture reveals that true financial stability comes from diligence, patience, and consistency, not taking shortcuts or making hasty decisions.

Proverbs 14:23 (NKJV) reinforces this by saying, "*In all labor there is profit, but idle chatter leads only to poverty.*" Talking about success, wishing for wealth, or even praying for financial breakthrough without taking action will not produce results. Profit comes from actual work, whether that is managing finances wisely, developing valuable skills, or building a business with patience. Financial success does not come from empty dreams or mere conversations but from faithful labor and discipline.

The contrast between wisdom and foolishness in financial matters is made clear in Proverbs 10:4 (NKJV), which states, "*He who has a slack hand becomes poor, but the hand of the diligent makes rich.*" Laziness in financial stewardship, whether that means neglecting to budget, refusing to plan, or ignoring wise investment strategies, leads to lack. Conversely, those who work diligently, stay consistent in their financial habits, and refuse to be complacent will see increase. Money flows to those who are prepared to handle it, while those who lack discipline and accountability often struggle to hold onto wealth, no matter how much they earn.

Proverbs 13:4 (NKJV) further elaborates on this principle, saying, "*The soul of a lazy man desires, and has nothing; but the soul of the diligent shall be made rich.*" Many people want financial breakthrough, but their actions do not align with their desires. They want success, but they are unwilling to take the necessary steps of learning, growing, managing, and making sacrifices for long-term gain. The lazy man desires wealth but never attains it because he refuses to embrace the consistent habits and the effort required to sustain it. The diligent man, however, may not see immediate results, but through faithful action, he is steadily positioned for prosperity.

The truth is, money does not simply follow desire, it follows discipline. Wanting more money, praying for financial breakthroughs, or even working hard is not enough if there is no structure, planning, and wisdom behind it. Those who apply diligence in every area of financial stewardship by budgeting, saving, investing, and giving, will experience steady increase. However, those who refuse to plan, spend recklessly, or rely on impulsive decisions will continue to struggle. God is a God of order, and financial success follows those who steward His resources with wisdom, patience, and discipline.

A Legacy of Faithful Finances

Nathan had always been a hard worker. From the moment he landed his first job, he was determined to be financially successful. He had seen his parents consistently struggle to make ends meet, living paycheck to paycheck, constantly burdened by debt. He promised himself that his life would be different. He read every financial book he could find, followed investment trends, and absorbed every strategy the world had to offer on how to build wealth.

By the time he was thirty-five, Nathan had achieved what many would consider financial success. He owned a beautiful home, drove a luxury car, had multiple investments, and a growing savings account. Yet, despite all his financial wisdom, he felt restless. No matter how much money he made, he always felt like he was just one bad decision away from losing it all.

One day, during a conversation with his mentor, Pastor James, Nathan shared his frustrations.

"I work hard, I save, I invest," Nathan said. "Yet, no matter how much I earn, I never feel secure. I'm always thinking about the next opportunity, the next investment, the next financial goal."

Pastor James leaned back in his chair and smiled. "Nathan, tell me something, who owns your money?"

Nathan frowned. "I do. I earned it."

"That's your first problem," Pastor James replied. "You think your money belongs to you. You don't own anything; you are simply a steward of what God has given you. Until you see money through God's eyes, you will always feel unsettled."

Nathan sat quietly as Pastor James opened his Bible.

*"The borrower **is** servant to the lender."* (Proverbs 22:7, NKJV)

"You have no debt, right?" Pastor James asked.

Nathan shook his head. "No, I've worked hard to stay debt-free."

"That's good," Pastor James nodded. "Most people don't realize that debt is bondage. When you owe money, you are working for someone else, not for God's Kingdom. Debt keeps people enslaved to jobs they don't love and businesses they don't believe in, simply because they need to make payments. Financial freedom isn't just about avoiding debt, it's about making sure that money is serving you, not the other way around."

Pastor James then turned to 2 Kings 4:2 (NKJV), where the prophet Elisha asked the widow, *"Tell me, what do you have in the house?"*

"She thought she had nothing," Pastor James explained, "but God had already given her a resource that could be multiplied. So many people pray for financial breakthrough when the provision is already in their hands. They just don't recognize it."

Nathan's mind started racing. He had been so focused on chasing wealth that he had never thought about what God had already placed in his life. He had skills, knowledge, and resources that he hadn't even considered as ways to create impact. He had been so focused on getting more money that he had ignored the opportunities to multiply what he already had.

"This is where many people go wrong," he said. "They desire wealth, but they don't plan for it. They chase quick profits, risky investments, and shortcuts, hoping for overnight success. God blesses those who are diligent, consistent, and patient."

Nathan thought about all the times he had jumped on investment trends, hoping to make quick money. Some worked, but others failed. Instead of focusing on sustainable growth, wise planning, and steady progress, he had been running after short-term gains.

Pastor James smiled, "Money follows discipline, not desire. Hard work, persistence, and faithful stewardship create increase, not wishful thinking."

"It's not enough to want financial success," he continued. "Many people talk about wealth, but they never take real action. They waste time making excuses instead of making progress. Faithful financial management requires action, real steps toward discipline, consistency, and wisdom."

By now, Nathan was deep in thought. He had always believed that as long as he managed his money wisely, he was doing the right thing. But something was still unsettled in his heart.

Then, Pastor James turned to 1 Timothy 6:10 which states:

"For the love of money is a root of all kinds of evil, for which some have strayed from the faith in their greediness, and pierced themselves through with many sorrows." (NKJV)

Nathan swallowed hard. "Are you saying it's wrong to make money?"

"Not at all," Pastor James reassured him. "Money is not evil, but the *love* of money is. The moment your security, identity, and peace are tied to how much money you have, you have made wealth your master. God gives wealth as a tool for impact, not as something to be worshiped."

Nathan realized that while he had stayed out of debt, saved, and invested, he had placed his trust in money, not in God. He had unknowingly made wealth his security. That was why he never felt peace, because money was controlling him, not the other way around.

"Wealth is for impact," he said. "God does not bless people financially just so they can live in luxury. He blesses them so they can bless others. Money is not meant to be stored up just for personal gain; it is meant to be used for Kingdom work, for helping those in need, for creating opportunities for others."

Nathan felt a shift in his heart. For years, he had seen money as something to build and protect for himself, but he had never thought about it as a tool for impact. He realized that true financial freedom is not just about having more, it is about using what God gives wisely, generously, and purposefully.

That conversation changed Nathan's life. From that day forward, he no longer saw himself as the owner of his wealth, he saw himself as a steward.

He stopped making decisions based on fear and started trusting God with what was already in his hands. Instead of chasing the next big investment, he built with diligence and discipline. Instead of placing his trust in money, he put his security in God, knowing that true financial peace comes not from what is in your bank account, but from who is Lord over your finances.

Nathan didn't stop making money. In fact, his wealth grew even more. However now, instead of hoarding it, he used it for Kingdom impact. For the first time, he felt at peace. Not because he had more money, but because he had finally aligned his finances with God's principles, God's purpose, and God's will.

Nathan's story is not just his, it is a lesson for anyone who desires financial success. Are you chasing money, or are you stewarding it? Is your security in wealth, or is it in God? Are you using your finances to serve the Kingdom, or are they simply serving you?

True prosperity is not just about how much you earn, it is about how well you manage what God entrusts to you. When you align your finances with God's principles, you step into freedom, increase, and purpose-driven wealth that outlives you, leaving a true Kingdom legacy.

The question is: Are you ready to steward money God's way?

Biblical Principles of Faithful Finances

The foundation of financial faithfulness is not in how much money you have but in how well you steward what God has entrusted to you. Money is a tool, not a master. When finances are aligned with biblical principles, they bring freedom, impact, and Kingdom expansion. The following principles are essential for managing money God's way:

1. **Avoid unnecessary debt.** – *"The borrower is servant to the lender."* (Proverbs 22:7, NKJV)

   Debt places a person under financial bondage, limiting their ability to invest, give, and move when God calls them. The world normalizes borrowing, but Scripture warns that unnecessary debt leads to servitude. Wise stewardship requires living within one's means, making careful financial decisions, and avoiding debt that creates long-term burdens.

2. **Trust what God has already given you.** – *"Tell me, what do you have in the house?"* (2 Kings 4:2, NKJV)

   Many believe they need more money to experience financial breakthrough, yet God often provides through what is already in our hands. The widow in 2 Kings 4 thought she had nothing, but her small jar of oil became the key to her financial freedom. Increase starts with recognizing, stewarding, and multiplying what God has already provided.

3. **Discipline creates wealth, not desire.** – *"The plans of the diligent lead surely to plenty, but those of everyone who is hasty, surely to poverty."* (Proverbs 21:5, NKJV)

Financial success is not the result of wishing, hoping, or impulsive decisions—it follows diligence, planning, and patience. Many desire wealth but lack the discipline to budget, save, invest, and steward resources wisely. Those who consistently apply financial wisdom will see increase, while those who rush into financial decisions without strategy will struggle.

4. **Hard work and persistence bring results.** – *"In all labor there is profit, but idle chatter leads only to poverty."* (Proverbs 14:23, NKJV)

Many people talk about financial success but never take action. Planning and talking are not enough, wealth is created through consistent effort and faithful work. Those who commit to learning, growing, and taking intentional steps toward financial wisdom will experience lasting prosperity.

5. **Wealth follows preparation and consistency.** – *"The soul of a lazy man desires, and has nothing; but the soul of the diligent shall be made rich."* (Proverbs 13:4, NKJV)

Many people want financial increase but are unwilling to put in the time, effort, and discipline required to sustain it. God honors those who work with diligence and remain faithful in their financial stewardship. Laziness leads to lack, but perseverance leads to provision.

6. **Money should serve God, not control you.** – *"The love of money is a root of all kinds of evil."* (1 Timothy 6:10, NKJV)

Money itself is not evil, but when it becomes an idol, it leads to greed, fear, and misplaced trust. Some chase after money at the expense of their faith, family, and integrity, while others hoard wealth out of fear instead of trusting God. Money should never be the source of security, God is. When wealth is submitted to Him, it becomes a tool for His purposes, not a distraction from His presence.

7. **Wealth is for impact.** – *"He who has pity on the poor lends to the LORD, and He will pay back what he has given."* (Proverbs 19:17, NKJV)

True prosperity is not about accumulation but about impact. God blesses financial stewardship so that His people can give, serve, and expand His Kingdom. Those who manage money wisely will not only experience increase but will also be positioned to be a blessing to others.

Applying These Principles:

- Avoid unnecessary debt. Live within your means, make wise financial choices, and refuse to be enslaved by debt that limits your ability to give and invest in God's Kingdom.

- Trust what God has already given you. Recognize and steward the resources you currently have, knowing that financial breakthrough often comes through what is already in your hands.

- Discipline creates wealth, not desire. Commit to budgeting, saving, and making strategic financial decisions rather than relying on impulsive spending or wishful thinking.

- Hard work and persistence bring results. Stop waiting for financial success and take intentional, consistent action toward wise money management.

- Wealth follows preparation and consistency. Develop long-term financial habits, stay diligent in your work, and trust that God honors faithfulness in stewardship.

- Money should serve God, not control you. View money as a tool for Kingdom impact, never allowing it to dictate your decisions, priorities, or sense of security.

- Wealth is for impact. Use financial increase as an opportunity to give generously, help others, and expand God's Kingdom rather than hoarding it for personal gain.

The way you handle money today determines the level of increase and influence God can entrust to you tomorrow. Faithful financial management is not just about getting out of debt or making wise investments, it is about aligning your finances with God's Kingdom agenda. Money follows those who are disciplined, diligent, and willing to steward every resource with integrity and purpose.

Many people pray for financial breakthrough while ignoring the Kingdom principles that bring lasting increase. Yet, breakthrough is not always about receiving more, it is about being faithful with what is already in your hands. The widow in 2 Kings 4 did not receive a gift of money; she received a strategy for multiplication. God is calling you to manage your finances in a way that produces lasting fruit, not just temporary relief.

Wealth is not measured by what you accumulate, it is measured by what you are entrusted with because of your faithfulness. When you master the principles of biblical money management, financial freedom is no longer a distant hope but an expected outcome. The question is, will you continue to follow the world's system of debt, greed, and financial instability, or will you step into God's divine order for increase?

The next chapter will take you deeper into building sustainable, Kingdom-driven wealth, the kind that outlives you and impacts generations to come. You are not just called to manage money; you are called to multiply it for a purpose. If you are ready to move from financial survival to true financial stewardship, let's continue the journey. Your legacy of increase starts now.

Part 4

TAKING ACTION & BUILDING LASTING PROSPERITY

You've come a long way on this journey, and the fact that you're still here means you are serious about aligning your life and business with God's principles. Many desire success, but few take the time to build it on a foundation that will last. What you are learning is not just about making more money or growing a business, it is about establishing a legacy of prosperity, stewardship, and impact that is proven in the Word of God.

Everything up to this point has been about renewing your mindset, shifting your perspective on wealth, and learning the biblical principles that govern financial increase. Now, it is time to take action. This final section will equip you with the strategy, wisdom, and faith to build something that outlives you. You will learn how to break free from the limitations of a poverty mindset, step into Kingdom-driven wealth, and establish a foundation that will continue to prosper for generations.

The truth is, God does not just want you to succeed temporarily. He wants you to build something that will make an impact long after you are gone. A business that reflects His wisdom. A financial system that operates on His principles. A legacy that transforms lives. Too many people work hard only to leave behind nothing of lasting value. That will not be your story.

Now is the time to take everything you've learned and put it into action. You were not designed for mediocrity; you were designed to prosper. Are you ready to step into the fullness of what God has for you? Let's move forward.

10

OVERCOMING FEAR & TAKING RISKS IN FAITH

Fear is one of the greatest barriers to success while faith is the key that unlocks the door to prosperity. Every great move of God requires stepping into the unknown, trusting Him beyond what is visible, and believing what He has spoken even when circumstances appear otherwise. The difference between those who walk in supernatural increase and those who stay stagnant is not talent, resources, or intelligence, it is faith.

God commands His people not to fear, not as a suggestion, but as a requirement to walk in His promises. Joshua 1:9 states: *"Have I not commanded you? Be strong and of good courage; do not be afraid, nor be dismayed, for the LORD your God is with you wherever you go."* (NKJV). This verse is not simply encouragement, it is a command to step forward boldly, knowing that God is always with you. He is for you and not against you.

Many people wait, hoping for fear to disappear before taking action. However, faith is not the absence of fear, it is the decision to move forward despite it. Fear will always attempt to limit you, but courage is choosing to trust God beyond what you can control through your own strength.

Fear is not from God. It is an attack from the enemy designed to keep you from stepping into His purpose. 2 Timothy 1:7 confirms this truth:

"For God has not given us a spirit of fear, but of power and of love and of a sound mind." (NKJV)

This verse reveals three powerful truths. First, fear is not from God, it is a tool of the enemy to paralyze progress. Second, God has already given power, love, and a sound mind as replacements for fear. Power means the ability to overcome obstacles, love means complete confidence in God's faithfulness, and a sound mind means clarity and peace in decision-making.

Fear thrives where faith is absent. When fear is allowed to control decisions, it keeps people stuck in doubt, hesitation, and inaction. The only way to overcome fear is to fill yourself with faith, through prayer, the Word, and bold action.

Emotions Are a Tool, Not a Master

God created emotions. Jesus Himself experienced joy, sorrow, anger, and deep compassion. Emotions were given to us as signals, not as a foundation for decision-making.

Hebrews 4:15 states, *"For we do not have a High Priest who cannot sympathize with our weaknesses, but was in all points tempted as we are, yet without sin."* (NKJV). Jesus felt emotions deeply, yet He was never ruled by them.

In the Garden of Gethsemane, Jesus experienced deep distress before going to the cross. He acknowledged His emotions, but He submitted to the will of the Father. *"Father, if it is Your will, take this cup away from Me; nevertheless not My will, but Yours, be done."* (Luke 22:42, NKJV).

This is an example of faith in action. Fear, worry, and doubt may come, but they should never dictate our decisions. A person who builds their life upon emotions will always be unstable, but a person who builds their life on faith will see growth, success, and lasting impact.

The Relationship Built in Total Dependence on God

Faith grows deepest in seasons where there is no backup plan, no safety net, only God. When human effort is no longer enough, faith is the only option.

Abraham left his home for an unknown land without a clear destination. Moses stretched out his hand over the Red Sea before it parted. Peter walked on water not because it made sense but because he trusted Jesus' call. Each of these individuals saw the miraculous because they chose faith over fear.

True intimacy with God is developed in the moments where faith is all that remains. When there is nothing left but trust, God proves Himself faithful in ways beyond imagination. The greatest testimonies are born in the places where logic ends, and faith begins.

The world teaches self-reliance, but Kingdom success requires God-reliance. Faith is the key that unlocks supernatural provision, favor, and increase. Every major breakthrough in Scripture was preceded by an act of faith. Those who trust God fully will always see His hand move in ways that defy natural limits.

Big Faith Leads to Big Impact

The level of faith displayed determines the level of impact. Those who think small, dream small, and believe small will see small results. God never called anyone to mediocrity, He called them to expansion, multiplication, and dominion.

Faith-filled entrepreneurs build businesses that influence nations. Faith-driven leaders step into places of power that shift cultures. Those who trust God with boldness leave legacies that last for generations. Nothing great is accomplished through hesitation. Big faith unlocks supernatural results, expands influence, and brings transformation beyond personal gain. Faith is not just about believing, it is about stepping out when there are no guarantees except God's Word. When faith is acted upon, the supernatural is activated.

Growth Requires Stepping Outside the Comfort Zone

Comfort is the enemy of progress and prosperity. Nothing significant happens inside a comfort zone. Those who refuse to step into discomfort will never experience the fullness of their potential.

Jesus constantly called His disciples into situations that stretched their faith. Peter walked on water only after stepping out of the boat. The five thousand were fed only when the disciples took what little they had and put it in Jesus' hands. Miracles followed obedience that required discomfort along with the stretching of their faith.

In business, leadership, and finances, growth always comes outside the familiar. Staying in the same patterns, routines, and limited thinking will always produce the same results. Expansion requires stepping into the unknown, learning new skills, making bold decisions, and trusting God in ways never done before.

Proverbs 3:5-6 states, *"Trust in the LORD with all your heart, and lean not on your own understanding; in all your ways acknowledge Him, and He shall direct your paths."* (NKJV). Growth comes when faith is placed in God rather than human reasoning. The moment a person refuses to step beyond what they can control, they limit what God can truly do in their life.

Fear That Holds You Back VS Faith That Propels You Forward

Fear will always give reasons to stay where it feels safe. It will whisper that now is not the right time, that failure is too likely, that staying where you are is better than the unknown. Faith, however, moves forward despite fear. Faith steps out when nothing is certain except God's promise. Faith understands that increase follows obedience, and God never calls someone without equipping them for what is ahead.

Fear will say, *"What if I fail?"*

Faith will respond, *"What if God moves beyond what I can imagine?"*

Fear will say, *"I'm not ready."*

Faith will respond, *"God qualifies the called, not the other way around."*

Fear will say, *"This is too big for me."*

Faith will respond, *"Nothing is too big for God."*

Everything God has for you lies on the other side of faith. Growth will never come by staying where it's comfortable. The next level of prosperity, leadership, and success is waiting for those bold enough to take risks in faith.

God does not expect perfection, He expects obedience. The world's system teaches playing it safe, waiting until everything is secure. God's system rewards those who step forward when all they have is His Word. Faith opens doors that human effort never could. The choice is yours, stay where it's safe, or step into the unknown where God's abundance awaits.

This journey is not for the fearful but for the faithful. The next chapter will take this to another level, unlocking how to make Spirit-led decisions that will set you apart as a leader in business, finance, and life. If you are ready to walk in fearless faith, it's time to move forward. Your next level is waiting!

A Story of Overcoming Fear & Taking Risks in Faith

Ava sat at her desk, staring at the contract on her laptop screen. The cursor blinked at her like a countdown clock, daring her to take the next step. If she signed, everything would change. If she walked away, she could return to the safety of what she knew, her stable but unfulfilling corporate job. Her heart pounded. She had prayed for this moment, dreamed of it, and worked for it. Now that it was in front of her, fear gripped her like heavy iron chains.

"What if I fail?"

"What if this business doesn't work?"

"What if I lose everything?"

Ava had always played it safe. She grew up in a home where security was valued above all else. Her parents worked steady jobs, paid their bills on time, and never took risks. To them, stability was success, and for a while, she believed it too.

She had followed the "safe" path, graduating from college, landing a well-paying job, climbing the corporate ladder. Yet, every day felt like she was suffocating. Sitting in meetings that drained her, working long hours for someone else's dream, and feeling like she was created for more but too afraid to go after it. Then one day God had given her an idea.

A vision for a business that would allow her to use her gifts, impact people's lives, and create financial freedom. At first, she dismissed it as an unrealistic dream. However, the idea wouldn't leave her. It woke her up at night. It stirred her spirit in the middle of work meetings. It was as if God was asking her, *"Will you trust Me? Will you step out in faith?"*

She had spent months preparing, learning, saving, and networking to lay the groundwork. She thought she was ready. Now, with the opportunity in front of her, fear roared louder than faith.

Ava leaned back in her chair, rubbing her temples.

Fear whispered:
"This is a mistake. Stay where it's safe."
"You're not qualified. You don't have what it takes."
"What if you step out and fail in front of everyone?"

Faith, though quieter, spoke with certainty:

"Have I not commanded you? Be strong and of good courage; do not be afraid, nor be dismayed, for the LORD your God is with you wherever you go." (Joshua 1:9, NKJV)

She closed her eyes and took a deep breath. She had read that verse before, but today, it felt like a direct message from God. Fear was not from Him.

"For God has not given us a spirit of fear, but of power and of love and of a sound mind." (2 Timothy 1:7, NKJV)

Fear was trying to keep her small. Trying to keep her stuck. Trying to keep her from stepping into everything God had prepared for her. Ava grabbed her Bible from the shelf, flipping through the pages. Her eyes landed on the story of Peter walking on water.

"Lord, if it is You, command me to come to You on the water."

"So He said, 'Come.' And when Peter had come down out of the boat, he walked on the water to go to Jesus." (Matthew 14:28-29, NKJV)

Peter walked on water only when he stepped out of the boat. She slammed the Bible shut. Faith was action. Faith meant moving even when the outcome wasn't guaranteed. Faith meant stepping out. Ava stood up, pacing the room. She had spent her whole life waiting for the "right time," the "perfect conditions," the guarantee that it would all work out, but faith doesn't work like that. Faith is moving forward when fear tells you to stay frozen, stuck where you are. Faith is trusting God when logic says it's impossible. Faith is knowing that you will never walk on water if you refuse to leave the boat. Ava sat down, took one last deep breath, and clicked "Sign." A wave of nervous excitement rushed through her. It was done. She had taken the leap. She wasn't just hoping for success anymore, she was stepping into it.

The Growth That Comes from Discomfort

The next few months tested Ava in ways she never imagined. She faced obstacles she didn't see coming. There were days when doubt crept back in, when money was tight, when she questioned if she had made a mistake. Yet, in every moment of uncertainty, God showed up.

Clients began to find her. Opportunities opened that she hadn't even pursued. Resources came just when she needed them. Through it all, her faith grew deeper than it had ever been before. She realized something powerful: growth never happens in comfort. If she had stayed in her job, she would have never discovered what she was capable of. If she had let fear win, she would have never experienced the joy of walking in her purpose. The business didn't just grow, she grew. She became bold. Confident. A leader. A woman of faith who no longer lived in the shadows of fear.

Ava's story is not just hers, it can be yours too. Maybe you've been feeling that same pull. That nudge from God to step into something new. To start the business. To take the risk. To trust Him for more. Maybe, like Ava, fear has kept you stuck up until now. This is your moment.

Fear will always be there. It will always try to hold you back. You have a choice though. Will you let fear control you, or will you step out in faith? God is calling you to a life beyond your comfort zone. A life where your faith leads to impact. A life where Kingdom risks lead to Kingdom rewards. You will never grow if you refuse to move. You will never see miracles if you stay in the boat. It's time to take the leap. Your faith-filled future is waiting!

Biblical Principles of Overcoming Fear & Taking Risks in Faith

Faith is the foundation of every breakthrough, every promotion, and every supernatural move of God. Fear keeps people stagnant, but faith moves them forward into the promises of God. Stepping out in faith requires trusting in God's direction rather than relying on comfort, security, or personal understanding. The following biblical principles will reinforce the truths covered in this chapter, ensuring that you build a life and business rooted in courage, boldness, and complete trust in God.

1. **God commands courage, not fear.** – *"Have I not commanded you? Be strong and of good courage; do not be afraid, nor be dismayed, for the LORD your God is with you wherever you go."* (Joshua 1:9, NKJV)

   o Fear is not just an emotion, it is something God commands us to reject. Courage is a choice to move forward, knowing that God has already gone before you.

2. **Fear is not from God; power, love, and a sound mind are.** – *"For God has not given us a spirit of fear, but of power and of love and of a sound mind."* (2 Timothy 1:7, NKJV)

   o Fear is a tool of the enemy to keep you small. God has already given you the power to overcome, the love to trust Him, and the clarity to make wise decisions.

3. **Emotions are given for awareness, but they are not meant to lead us in our decisions.** – *"For we do not have a High Priest who cannot sympathize with our weaknesses, but was in all points tempted as we are, yet without sin."* (Hebrews 4:15, NKJV)

   o Jesus experienced emotions, yet He never allowed them to dictate His actions. Faith moves beyond emotions and follows truth.

4. **Faith is built in total dependence on God.** – *"Trust in the LORD with all your heart, and lean not on your own understanding; in all your ways acknowledge Him, and He shall direct your paths."* (Proverbs 3:5-6, NKJV)

o The greatest faith is developed when there is nothing left but trust in God. The more you depend on Him, the greater the increase and breakthroughs you will see.

5. **Faith produces supernatural impact.** – *"Jesus said to him, 'If you can believe, all things are possible to him who believes.'"* (Mark 9:23, NKJV)

   o The size of your faith determines the size of your results. Small faith limits what God can do in your life; bold faith unlocks the impossible.

6. **Growth only happens outside of comfort.** – *"Enlarge the place of your tent, and let them stretch out the curtains of your dwellings; do not spare; lengthen your cords, and strengthen your stakes."* (Isaiah 54:2, NKJV)

   o Expansion requires stretching. You cannot stay in the same place doing the exact same things and expect different results. Growth happens when you step into new territory, take risks, and trust God fully.

7. **Fear will hold you back, while faith will propel you forward.** – *"For we walk by faith, not by sight."* (2 Corinthians 5:7, NKJV)

   o Faith is not about what you see, it is about what God has spoken. If you only move when things look secure, you will never experience the fullness of God's promises.

Applying These Principles

- God commands courage, not fear. Choose to step forward in faith, knowing that God has already gone before you to prepare the way.

- Fear is not from God; power, love, and a sound mind are. Reject fear, knowing that God has equipped you with everything you need to walk in boldness.

- Emotions are given for awareness, but they are not meant to lead you in your decisions. Acknowledge your emotions but allow faith, not feelings, to dictate your actions.

- Faith is built in total dependence on God. Trust God completely, even when you don't understand, and He will guide your path.

- Faith produces supernatural impact. The greater your faith, the greater the breakthroughs and opportunities God will release in your life.

- Growth only happens outside of comfort. Be willing to stretch, take risks, and step into new opportunities, trusting God for the outcome.

- Fear will hold you back, while faith will propel you forward. Move based on what God has spoken, not on what your circumstances currently look like.

You are not here by accident. You are not reading this book by coincidence. God has brought you to this very moment because He is calling you to step into something greater. The dreams in your heart, the ideas that won't leave you, the deep desire for more, they are not random. They are placed in you by the One who created you for purpose, impact, and influence.

For far too long, fear has tried to keep you from moving forward. It has whispered lies of doubt, insecurity, and hesitation. It has convinced you to stay where it feels safe, where you are in control. Yet deep down, you know you were never meant to stay in the shallow waters.

This is your moment. God is calling you higher. He is challenging you to break free from fear, to take the leap of faith, to trust Him like never before. The next level of your life, your business, and your destiny is waiting for you to step forward in boldness.

Fear will always try to speak, but now you know the truth: God has not given you a spirit of fear, but of power, love, and a sound mind. (2 Timothy 1:7, NKJV)

He is with you, He has gone before you, and He will never leave you. The same God who parted the Red Sea, who led Peter to walk on water, and who took David from the fields to the throne, is the same God who is leading you now. Do not wait for the perfect conditions. Do not sit back hoping fear will disappear before you move. Faith is a decision, not a feeling. This is your time to rise. This is your moment to say yes. This is the season where you silence fear, step out of the boat, and walk boldly into the life God has destined for you.

The next chapter will take you deeper into making Spirit-led decisions that will set you apart as a leader in business, finances, and life. You were born for this. You were created to win. You were designed to prosper. Now go. Step forward. Your destiny is waiting!

11

BUILDING GENERATIONAL WEALTH

Wealth, wisdom, and faith are never meant to stop with one generation. Everything God entrusts to you, your knowledge, business, financial increase, and influence is meant to be passed down, multiplied, and sustained for those who come after you. A true legacy is not just about leaving behind financial assets; it is about imparting a Kingdom mindset, values, and faith that create lasting prosperity for generations to come.

Proverbs 13:22 states, *"A good man leaves an inheritance to his children's children, but the wealth of the sinner is stored up for the righteous."* (NKJV). This verse reveals that wealth generated with Kingdom wisdom is designed to outlive you. Short-sighted financial decisions, lack of proper planning, and poor stewardship often cause wealth to be lost within one generation. However, those who build with a generational mindset understand that they are not just working for today, but for their children and their children's children.

A person's greatest investment is not in stocks, real estate, or businesses, it is in the people they are called to influence, lead and train. If a fortune is built but the next generation is not taught how to manage, multiply, and steward it, that wealth will simply be wasted or squandered. Money alone does not create prosperity; a transformed and renewed Kingdom mindset does. If a person inherits wealth but has a poverty mindset, they will mismanage and deplete their resources. If a person is taught to have a wealth-building, faith-driven mindset, they will multiply what is given to them, creating lasting impact and expansion.

The Foundation of a Lasting Legacy

Building generational success starts with what is instilled, not just what is given. Proverbs 19:14 states, *"Houses and riches are an inheritance from fathers, but a prudent wife is from the Lord."* (NKJV). This verse shows that financial wealth can be passed down, but true wisdom and discernment are from God.

An inheritance that is purely financial will fade. While an inheritance that includes wisdom, principles, and the ability to create, steward, and multiply wealth will stand the test of time. Too many families have lost generational wealth because they focused on giving riches but failed to transfer the knowledge and Kingdom values required to sustain the wealth. A financial foundation without wisdom is like a house built on sand, it will not withstand the storms of economic downturns, unexpected losses, or mismanagement.

Every successful business owner, entrepreneur, or leader must ask themselves: *What am I teaching the next generation?* Am I just handing them financial wealth, or am I training them in discipline, a strong work ethic, faith, and financial stewardship so they will know how to continue to build upon what I leave behind?

Teaching the Next Generation

Psalm 78:5-7 states, *"For He established a testimony in Jacob, and appointed a law in Israel, which He commanded our fathers, that they should make them known to their children; that the generation to come might know them, the children who would be born, that they may arise and declare them to their children, that they may set their hope in God, and not forget the works of God, but keep His commandments."* (NKJV).

118

This scripture reveals the blueprint for generational success. It begins with teaching, training, and intentional leadership. Just as faith must be passed down, so must the Kingdom principles of stewardship, integrity, and wealth creation. Children must be taught how to handle money, how to think generationally, how to build businesses with excellence, and how to trust God as their source.

Generational wealth does not start with financial gain, it starts with shifting the mindset from survival to stewardship, from consumption to creation, from spending to investing. A child who grows up seeing diligence, discipline, and generosity will naturally apply those principles when they become adults. (Proverbs 22:6) A child who only inherits wealth without understanding how to sustain it will be at risk of repeating the cycle of financial failure.

Legacy is established through consistent, intentional training. It is speaking over the next generation, declaring God's promises over them, and ensuring they have the tools to prosper beyond what you have built. It is reminding them to set their hope in God, to operate with integrity, and to never forget the Kingdom principles that create lasting prosperity.

God's Covenant of Generational Blessing

Genesis 17:7 states, *"And I will establish My covenant between Me and you and your descendants after you in their generations, for an everlasting covenant, to be God to you and your descendants after you."* (NKJV).

God's covenant with Abraham was not just for him, it was for every generation after him. Every promise of increase, multiplication, and divine provision was meant to continue beyond one lifetime. The same is true for every Kingdom-minded entrepreneur, leader, and parent. We are not just called to build businesses for personal success; we are called to build generationally. This means making financial and business decisions with the future in mind, not just considering what works for today, but what will sustain for decades to come.

God blesses obedience, not just ambition. The most successful business leaders are not just those who achieve great things in their lifetime, but those who set up the next generation for continued success. True prosperity is not about how much is gained in a single lifetime, but about how much wisdom and faithfulness are transferred to those who come after.

Success is Obedience, Not Just Achievement

The world measures success by accomplishments, titles, and wealth. However, true success is not just about what is built, it is about whether or not it was built in obedience to God. A business, financial empire, or personal fortune means nothing if it is not aligned with Kingdom principles and God's purpose.

Many people chase financial gain, believing that the more they acquire, the more successful they are. Yet, God's standard of success is different. He calls His people to build in a way that honors Him, through integrity, service, and stewardship.

Success without obedience is empty. Building wealth apart from God's principles may bring temporary gain, but it does not create eternal impact. Every financial decision, every business move, every investment should be made with the mindset of, *"Is this aligned with God's plan? Will this honor Him? Am I building something that will last beyond me?"*

The Mindset That Sustains Generational Wealth

A poverty mindset thinks only of today. A Kingdom mindset thinks in terms of generations. Those who build without a long-term vision often make decisions that serve immediate desires but do not create lasting prosperity. Those who understand the value of multiplication, investment, and Kingdom stewardship will establish businesses, financial legacies, and faith foundations that continue far beyond their lifetime.

Raising up the next generation begins with transforming the way wealth is viewed and managed. Financial literacy, stewardship, and faith-driven decision-making should be taught as early as possible. Children must see that money is a tool not an idol, and that it is meant to be used for advancing the Kingdom, providing for families, and creating opportunities for others.

Legacy-building requires vision beyond your own lifetime. The choices made today determine whether the next generation will thrive or struggle. Leaving a financial inheritance is good, but leaving a Kingdom mindset, a faith foundation, and a generational covenant with God is what creates true prosperity.

God is not just calling you to build for yourself, He is calling you to establish a foundation that will bless your children, grandchildren, and generations beyond what you can see today. Everything He gives is meant to be multiplied. Wealth, wisdom, and faith must be sown into the next generation so they can continue the work He started through you. A true Kingdom entrepreneur does not build for themselves alone. They build with eternity in mind. They build so that their children will not have to start over, but will have the knowledge, faith, and financial stability to go even further.

The next chapter will bring it all together, showing how to fully align your faith, business, and finances to establish a lasting impact that glorifies God. You are not just building for today, you are building for generations to come. The question is, what kind of legacy will you leave?

A Legacy Worth More Than Gold

David sat across from his father, staring at the old wooden desk that had been in their family for generations. It had scratches and worn spots from years of use, yet it carried stories of wisdom, faith, and perseverance. His father, Tom, was a self-made entrepreneur who built a successful business from the ground up. Now, in his late sixties, he was ready to pass the legacy on to David.

"Son," James said, folding his hands over the worn-out ledger in front of him, "this business is yours now. I've spent my life building it, but what I'm leaving you is not just a company, it's a legacy. The question is, will you sustain it, or will you let it slip away?"

David sighed, rubbing his temples. "Dad, I appreciate everything you've done, but the world is different now. Business is unpredictable, markets shift overnight, and success isn't guaranteed."

Tom nodded knowingly. "I get it. The world changes, but Kingdom principles do not. What built this company wasn't luck, it was faith, wisdom, and obedience to God's principles. If you follow them, this legacy won't just survive, it will multiply."

David had grown up watching his father work tirelessly, making wise decisions, taking calculated risks, and always seeking God's direction. The business had provided well for their family, but it wasn't just the financial stability that made an impact, it was the way his father built it.

Tom had instilled in David a strong work ethic. He always said, *"Wealth without wisdom is wasted."* He taught David to see money as a tool, not a master. He emphasized that the business was not just about making a profit but about honoring God and serving people.

As a child, David watched his father turn down lucrative deals that lacked integrity. He remembered how his father would pause and pray before making major financial decisions. He recalled the times Tom would tell his employees, "This business will never be built on dishonesty, no matter how much money is on the table."

David also saw how his father gave generously, not just to their family, but to others. He funded scholarships, supported single mothers in the church, and created opportunities for employees to grow and become leaders themselves.

Proverbs 13:22 echoed in David's mind: *"A good man leaves an inheritance to his children's children, but the wealth of the sinner is stored up for the righteous."* (NKJV).

His father was a good man. He wasn't just leaving behind a business; he was leaving behind a Kingdom mindset and foundation, and a way of living that honored God.

David had his own doubts. He had seen second-generation business owners fail to uphold the legacy given to them. He feared that he might make the wrong decisions, that he wouldn't be able to carry the weight of what his father built. Tom sensed his hesitation. "David, do you know what separates families that build generational wealth from those that lose it?"

David shook his head.

"It's not the amount of money they leave behind. It's the mindset they pass down. If you carry the same Kingdom mindset that built this, you won't just sustain it, you'll expand it. However, if you ignore the principles that created this legacy, it will crumble."

David thought about Proverbs 19:14: *"Houses and riches are an inheritance from fathers, but a prudent wife is from the Lord."* (NKJV). Wealth could be inherited, but wisdom had to be learned, given from the Lord (James 1:5). Without wisdom, an inheritance could be spent recklessly. Without knowledge, success would only be temporary.

His father had prepared him for this moment all his life, not by giving him everything, but rather by teaching him how to manage, steward, and multiply what was given to him.

Tom pulled out an old Bible from his desk. The pages were worn, filled with underlined verses and handwritten notes. "David, I've lived my life by these principles. When I started this business,

I made a covenant with God. I told Him that whatever He gave me, I would use to glorify Him, to bless my family, and to help others."

He flipped to Genesis 17:7, *"And I will establish My covenant between Me and you and your descendants after you in their generations, for an everlasting covenant, to be God to you and your descendants after you."* (NKJV).

"This business is not just about us," Tom continued. "God's promises are for generations. That means we don't just work for ourselves; we build something that carries impact beyond our lifetime."

David felt a shift inside him. He had been looking at this transition as a burden, when in reality, it was a privilege, a true blessing. He wasn't just inheriting a company, he was inheriting a calling. The world defined success as wealth, status, and achievement. His father had always defined success differently.

"David, success is not just about how much money you make. Success is obedience to God's instructions. If you seek Him first as the Bible tells us in Matthew 6:33, everything else will follow."

David thought about Psalm 78:5-7, which spoke of passing down God's ways to the next generation so that they might continue to walk in them:

"That they may set their hope in God, and not forget the works of God, but keep His commandments." (Psalm 78:7, NKJV).

His father had lived that out daily. He had built something on faith, obedience, and stewardship; something that wouldn't just last for years, but for generations. David took a deep breath and reached for the pen on the desk. He had a choice to make. He could take what his father had built and operate in fear, or he could step into it with faith, wisdom, and a commitment to follow the same principles which had created this legacy.

"Alright, Dad," he said with a smile. "I'm ready."

Tom leaned back in his chair, a look of peace washing over his face. "Good. Because this was never just about business. It's about fulfilling the assignment God has given us."

David walked out of that office with a new mindset. He would no longer fear the responsibility, he would embrace it. He would lead with integrity, trusting God in every decision, and teach his children the Kingdom same principles that had been instilled in him. Because legacy was never just about what was inherited, it was about what was built, sustained, and multiplied for generations to come.

Maybe you're at a place where you're thinking about what you're building, not just for yourself, but for those who come after you. Maybe fear has crept in, telling you that you're not equipped, that success is uncertain, or that building something lasting is too difficult.

Let this story be a reminder: Legacy is built by faith, wisdom, and obedience. It is not about how much you start with, but about the principles you apply to what you are given. You are building more than just wealth. You are creating a Kingdom foundation that will impact generations. Will you pass down wisdom, faith, and principles that will outlive you? Will you be the one who shifts the future of your family? God has given you everything you need to establish a generational legacy; will you use it wisely?

Biblical Principles of Building a Generational Legacy

True legacy is more than wealth, it is wisdom, faith, and principles that ensure success lasts for generations. The Bible provides a clear blueprint for building a foundation that not only blesses you but also impacts your children, grandchildren, and beyond. Below are the biblical principles that secure generational success, ensuring that what is built today continues to prosper in alignment with God's Word.

1. **A good man builds beyond his lifetime.** – *"A good man leaves an inheritance to his children's children, but the wealth*

of the sinner is stored up for the righteous." (Proverbs 13:22, NKJV)

> o True prosperity is not about short-term gain; it is about establishing something that lasts. A short-sighted approach focuses merely on personal success, but a Kingdom mindset ensures that what is built today continues to bless future generations.

2. **Wealth without wisdom will not last.** – *"Houses and riches are an inheritance from fathers, but a prudent wife is from the Lord."* (Proverbs 19:14, NKJV)

> o Money alone is not enough. Without wisdom, discipline, and a proper mindset, an inheritance can be wasted. Teaching the next generation how to steward and multiply resources ensures sustainability.

3. **Generational success requires intentional training.** – *"For He established a testimony in Jacob, and appointed a law in Israel, which He commanded our fathers, that they should make them known to their children; that the generation to come might know them, the children who would be born, that they may arise and declare them to their children, that they may set their hope in God, and not forget the works of God, but keep His commandments."* (Psalm 78:5-7, NKJV)

> o Legacy is not just about what is left behind, it is about what is taught, instilled, and modeled. A strong financial foundation must be accompanied by faith, wisdom, and biblical principles that ensure success continues through the generations.

4. **God's blessings and promises are generational.** – *"And I will establish My covenant between Me and you and your descendants after you in their generations, for an everlasting*

covenant, to be God to you and your descendants after you." (Genesis 17:7, NKJV)

- o God's blessings are not meant for just one person or one lifetime. His covenant extends to those who follow His ways. When financial success is built through obedience to His principles, it creates lasting impact that extends to future generations.

5. **Success is not just achievement, it is obedience.** – *"Commit your works to the LORD, and your thoughts will be established."* (Proverbs 16:3, NKJV)

- o The world defines success by status and wealth, but true success is alignment with God's will. Every decision, every business move, and every financial plan should be committed to Him. When obedience leads, success follows.

6. **Generational wealth requires a renewed mindset.** – *"Do not conform to the pattern of this world, but be transformed by the renewing of your mind."* (Romans 12:2, NIV)

- o The greatest inheritance is a renewed Kingdom mindset of stewardship, faith, and discipline. Teaching the next generation how to think about money, business, and leadership through a biblical lens ensures that what is given to them is not lost but multiplied.

7. **Faith and long-term vision sustain a legacy.** – *"For we walk by faith, not by sight."* (2 Corinthians 5:7, NKJV)

- o Building a lasting legacy requires seeing beyond the present. Many people focus only on immediate comfort, but those who think generationally create businesses, investments, and financial strategies that outlive them.

8. **Wisdom, not wealth, is the foundation of true prosperity.**
   – *"Through wisdom a house is built, and by understanding it is established; by knowledge the rooms are filled with all precious and pleasant riches."* (Proverbs 24:3-4, NKJV)

   o Financial inheritance is important, but wisdom is the key to sustaining it. Passing down wealth without teaching biblical financial principles is like giving someone you love a house with no foundation. Wisdom ensures that what is built today continues to prosper in the future.

Applying These Principles

- A good man builds beyond his lifetime. Focus on creating lasting impact, not just short-term success, by building with a Kingdom mindset.

- Wealth without wisdom will not last. Teach the next generation how to steward resources wisely, ensuring sustainability beyond your lifetime.

- Generational success requires intentional training. Instill faith, wisdom, and other biblical principles in your children to prepare them for long-term success.

- God's blessings and promises are generational. Walk in obedience to God's Word, knowing that His blessings extend to those who follow His ways.

- Success is not just achievement, it is obedience. Commit every business and financial decision to God, allowing Him to direct your path to true prosperity.

- Generational wealth requires a renewed mindset. Shift your thinking from short-term gains to long-term stewardship, teaching future generations to do the same.

- Faith and long-term vision sustain a legacy. Make decisions that align with God's plan, looking beyond the present to create impact for years to come.

- Wisdom, not wealth, is the foundation of true prosperity. Prioritize passing down biblical wisdom and financial stewardship over merely leaving material wealth to those who come after you.

Legacy is not just about what you leave, it is about who you prepare to carry it forward. The choices you make today will determine whether future generations thrive or struggle. What you build matters. Who you train and prepare to sustain it matters even more. God has given you everything you need to establish a generational legacy that is rooted in wisdom, faith, and stewardship. Will you build with eternity in mind? Will you pass down not just wealth, but the principles that sustain it? The next generation is waiting. Now is the time to build your Kingdom legacy.

12

SCALING YOUR BUSINESS WITH KINGDOM IMPACT

You have made it to the final chapter, and that alone is something to celebrate! You've invested your time, energy, and focus into something that has the potential to change your life forever. Many people start learning about Kingdom principles, but few commit to fully understanding and applying them. The fact that you've made it here means you are serious about building something that honors God, transforms lives, and establishes lasting impact.

Every principle, every strategy, and every biblical truth you've encountered in this book is not just knowledge, it is a divine invitation to step into your calling. The success you desire, the business you are called to build, and the impact you are meant to have are all within reach. Now, the next step is simple: Put it into action.

Scaling your business is not just about making more money or growing a larger platform. It is about multiplying the influence God has given you while staying firmly rooted in faith. True Kingdom impact is not just expansion, it is expansion with purpose, wisdom, and alignment with God's will.

Expanding Influence While Staying Rooted in Faith

Many people want to grow their businesses, expand their reach, and increase their wealth. Growth is good, but only if it is anchored in God's principles. The world teaches that success is about getting to the top as fast as possible, doing whatever it takes to increase revenue, and being seen by as many people as possible. God's Kingdom operates differently. Psalm 75:6-7 reminds us:

"For exaltation comes neither from the east nor from the west nor from the south. But God is the Judge: He puts down one and exalts another." (NKJV)

True promotion comes from God, and when He elevates you, nothing can bring you down. When you scale your business God's way, you don't have to rely on manipulation, shortcuts, or worldly tactics. Faithfulness, integrity, and obedience to His principles will position you for divine acceleration.

Matthew 6:33 declares, *"But seek first the kingdom of God and His righteousness, and all these things shall be added to you."* (NKJV). Scaling with Kingdom impact means God remains the foundation of everything you build. He is not an afterthought. Your faith does not shrink as your business grows, it strengthens. Your business is not just about financial gain. It is a tool for Kingdom expansion. Every product, service, or opportunity should be designed to serve others, meet needs, and transform lives. When you stay rooted in faith, your business becomes a platform where God moves, blesses, and impacts people beyond what you can imagine.

Your Business is a Ministry

Too often, people believe that ministry only happens in churches, on mission fields, or through global outreaches. While those are important, ministry is so much bigger than a title or an organization; it is a calling to serve wherever God places you.

Colossians 3:23-24 states, *"And whatever you do, do it heartily, as to the Lord and not to men, knowing that from the Lord you will receive the reward of the inheritance; for you serve the Lord Christ."* (NKJV).

If your business is doing the following, it is considered a ministry:

- If you are serving people, meeting needs, and conducting business with integrity, you are ministering.

- If you are building systems that create opportunities for others, you are ministering.

- If your business provides financial freedom for your family and enables you to give generously, you are ministering.

- If you are mentoring, coaching, or uplifting others through your work, you are ministering.

Ministry is not limited to preaching behind a pulpit, it is found in the day-to-day operations of a Kingdom-driven business. Your business is a place where people encounter the love of God, experience the excellence of His principles, and see His faithfulness in action.

Matthew 20:26-28 explains the heart of true leadership:

"Yet it shall not be so among you; but whoever desires to become great among you, let him be your servant. And whoever desires to be first among you, let him be your slave- just as the Son of Man did not come to be served, but to serve, and to give His life a ransom for many." (NKJV)

Business should not be about self-exaltation, it should be about service. Your business is an opportunity to bless others, create opportunities, and glorify God. Whether you employ people, mentor others, or simply provide products that improve lives, your business has the power to expand the Kingdom of God in ways you never imagined.

Now, This is Your Story

You've come to the final pages of this book, but this is not the end, it's the beginning. Now, this is your story.

You have walked through every principle, soaked up every biblical truth, and uncovered a new way of thinking about business, faith, and prosperity. The knowledge you have gained is more than just information, it is a divine strategy for your success.

You have everything you need. The blueprint is in your hands. The vision is in your heart. The next step is yours to take. For too long, you may have doubted, hesitated, or questioned whether you were truly called to build something meaningful. Those questions no longer limit you. You are chosen, equipped, and anointed to create, serve, and expand. Now, it's your time to take action.

Look at the vision God has placed inside of you. See the business, the team, the impact, the transformation. It's not just an idea, it's an assignment. God is calling you to build.

The fears that once held you back no longer have power over you. The doubt that once clouded your mind is now replaced with faith. Your business is not just a business, it is a ministry. Every product, every service, every transaction, and every client you serve is a part of a Kingdom assignment. This is not just about making money. This is about advancing God's purposes on the earth through what you create. So, what will you do next? Will you stay where it's safe, or will you step out in faith?

This is your Peter moment. The waves may be crashing. The winds may be blowing. The world may say it's too risky. But Jesus is calling you to step out of the boat. Walk on the water of faith. Build what He has placed in your heart. Trust Him for the results.

The time for waiting is over. The time for doubting is done. Now is the time to build. Now is the time to expand. Now is the time to walk boldly into the destiny God has set before you.

This is your story now. Go. Build. Serve. Prosper. The Kingdom is waiting for what God has placed inside of you, (Romans 8:19) and He is with you every step of the way. *It's time to rise!*

Biblical Principles of Scaling with Kingdom Impact

You have everything you need to step into your calling and build your business with Kingdom purpose. Scaling your business is not just about expansion, it's about multiplying impact, serving others, and staying rooted in faith. These biblical principles will guide you as you take the next steps forward in obedience to God's plan for your life and business.

1. **God has called you to build and expand.** – *"Enlarge the place of your tent, and let them stretch out the curtains of your dwellings; do not spare; lengthen your cords, and strengthen your stakes."* (Isaiah 54:2, NKJV)

   o Growth is part of God's design for His people. He doesn't call you to stay small. He calls you to expand your reach, increase your influence, and make an impact that outlives you.

2. **Your business is a ministry.** – *"And whatever you do, do it heartily, as to the Lord and not to men, knowing that from the Lord you will receive the reward of the inheritance; for you serve the Lord Christ."* (Colossians 3:23-24, NKJV)

   o Whether you are selling a product, providing a service, or leading a team, your business is an opportunity to serve God. Ministry is not just in the church, it's wherever people are being served and built up.

3. **Faith is required for expansion.** – *"For we walk by faith, not by sight."* (2 Corinthians 5:7, NKJV)

   o Scaling your business requires faith. You won't always see the full picture before you step out, but trusting God for provision and direction is key to supernatural growth.

4. **The greatest businesses are built on service.** – *"Yet it shall not be so among you; but whoever desires to become great among you, let him be your servant. And whoever desires to be first among you, let him be your slave—just as the Son of Man did not come to be served, but to serve, and to give His life a ransom for many."* (Matthew 20:26-28, NKJV)

   o Business is not just about revenue, it's about serving people well. When your focus is on meeting needs and adding value to others, expansion happens naturally.

5. **Seek first the Kingdom, and everything else will follow.** – *"But seek first the kingdom of God and His righteousness, and all these things shall be added to you."* (Matthew 6:33, NKJV)

   o If your business is truly aligned with Kingdom values, God will provide everything you need to grow.

6. **Success is obedience, not just achievement.** – *"Commit your works to the LORD, and your thoughts will be established."* (Proverbs 16:3, NKJV)

   o Growth should not be driven by worldly ambition, it should be rooted in obedience to God's direction. The real measure of success is faithfulness to your calling.

7. **God's favor brings supernatural increase.** – *"The blessing of the Lord makes one rich, and He adds no sorrow with it."* (Proverbs 10:22, NKJV)

   o When you build with integrity, faith, and obedience, God blesses your efforts in ways that human strategy alone cannot. His favor brings lasting prosperity without burden.

8. **Multiplication is a Kingdom principle.** – *"His lord said to him, 'Well done, good and faithful servant; you were faithful*

over a few things, I will make you ruler over many things. Enter into the joy of your lord.'" (Matthew 25:21, NKJV)

- o God rewards faithful stewardship with increase. If you manage what He has given you with excellence, He will entrust you with more.

Applying These Principles:

- God has called you to build and expand. Step out in faith, increase your influence, and build something that creates lasting impact.

- Your business is a ministry. View your business as a platform to serve others, glorify God, and advance His Kingdom through excellence.

- Faith is required for expansion. Trust God's provision and direction, even when the next steps aren't fully visible.

- The greatest businesses are built on service. Focus on meeting needs, solving problems, and adding value to others, and growth will follow.

- Seek first the Kingdom, and everything else will follow. Keep God as your foundation, and He will supply every resource you need.

- Success is obedience, not just achievement. Align your goals with God's will, and let faithfulness define your success.

- God's favor brings supernatural increase. Work with integrity, honor, and faith, and God will multiply your efforts far beyond what human ability alone could accomplish.

- Multiplication is a Kingdom principle. Steward what God has given you well, and He will entrust you with greater opportunities for impact.

Your Time to Prosper Starts Now

You have reached the end of this book, but this is far from the end of your journey. This is your launching point. You have been given the tools, the wisdom, and the divine strategies to step into everything God has prepared for you. No more hesitation. No more fear. No more waiting for the "perfect moment," because this is your moment.

God has called you to prosper, to build, to multiply, and to impact lives. Not for selfish gain, not for fleeting success, but for Kingdom purposes. Everything you have learned is not just information, it is revelation meant to be put into action. The seeds of greatness have already been planted in you. Now, it's time to cultivate them. It's time to water them with faith, diligence, and unwavering trust in God. The business you build, the wealth you steward, and the people you serve are all part of a greater plan, a Kingdom assignment that is bigger than you.

Faith Over Fear, Action Over Hesitation

For too long, fear has tried to keep you small. No more. You were never meant to live in limitation. You were never called to simply survive. You were designed to prosper. This is the moment where you decide:

Do you believe that God is your provider?

Will you trust that He has given you everything you need to succeed?

Will you walk in faith, knowing that His plans for you are good, abundant, and filled with purpose? Every great move of God begins with a step of obedience. What will your first step be?

Your Future is Waiting

Imagine one year from now. Five years from now. Ten years from now. Will you look back with regret, wishing you had trusted God more, wishing you had stepped out in faith? Or will you look back

138

in awe at how He multiplied your obedience and turned your faith into something far greater than you ever imagined? The choice is in front of you.

The time to build is **now**. The time to believe bigger, dream greater, and trust deeper is **now**. The time to step into prosperity, influence, and Kingdom impact is **now**.

God is waiting for your yes. Heaven is backing you. The resources, the connections, the wisdom, you already have access to through faith. All that's left to do is move.

You were made for this. You were designed to prosper. Now, go. Step into your destiny. Trust God like never before. Build with boldness. Serve with excellence. Walk in divine abundance. The Kingdom is waiting. ***Your time is now. Go. Build. Serve. Prosper.***

ABOUT THE AUTHOR

Maria Watkins is a devoted follower of Jesus, Kingdom entrepreneur, and the author of Hope Yet Again and How a Young Person Can Stay Pure. She is the founder of Empowered Legacy Ministries, where she equips and disciples entrepreneurs to step boldly into their God-given destinies. Through her ministry, Maria teaches believers to steward their businesses with faith, integrity, and biblical wisdom, aligning their success with God's divine purpose.

For over eight years, Maria's walk with God has been a testimony of healing, purpose, and unwavering faith. Through seasons of both trial and triumph, the Lord has revealed her true identity and ignited a passion to help others embrace the abundant life He has prepared for them. As a mother to two God-fearing young men, Maria considers it a privilege to lead her family in faith and inspire them to pursue their divine callings with courage and conviction.

Maria holds a Bachelor's degree in Computer Engineering and an Associate's degree in Design and Redesign, blending technical skills with creative insight. She further expanded her expertise by graduating from Bible College with a concentration in Financial Stewardship and completing advanced prophetic and apostolic training at RIG University. Her diverse educational background and personal journey of restoration uniquely position her to mentor faith-driven leaders, empowering them to prosper in their Kingdom assignments and make a lasting impact.

With a deep commitment to raising up resilient, purpose-driven individuals and families, especially single parents. Maria draws from her own story of perseverance to inspire others. She mentors Kingdom entrepreneurs to build businesses rooted in biblical principles and eternal impact. Her greatest joy is seeing others break free from limitations and step confidently into the extraordinary plans God has prepared for their lives.

Through every endeavor, Maria's mission remains clear: to equip leaders to prosper, overcome, and establish lasting Kingdom legacies.